Dusty Boots

My Dakota Cowboy Dad

A. Marlene Johnson

ISBN: 1448623308

To Dad
for telling me more

To Mom
for giving me the project

To Mom and Dad
for living my favorite love story

Willey Family Tree

Curtis Willey 1837-1927
   2 Absolum Day (Dode) Willey 1875-1959
      + Clara Luella Ellis 1875-1985
         3 Robert Curtis (R.C.) Willey 1910-1943
            + Letha Holtry
               4 Venita Eileen Willey
         3 Bonnie Marguerite Willey
            + Russell Steeves
         3 Gladys Marcelle Willey
            + James Jackson
               4 Max Russell Jackson
               4 Bonnie Karen Jackson
         3 Noble Day Willey
            + Margaret Mae French
               4 Dolyce Ann
               4 Jerry Dean
               4 Raymond Clare
               4 Larry Noble
         3 Orman Othe Willey
            + Emma Louise Ruby
               4 Valerie Faye
               4 Alyce Marlene
               4 Orman Ray
         3 Alden Ellis (Babe) Willey
            + Margo Anderson
               4 Allen Dennis
               4 Paulette Kay

Contents

Foreword

Along my journey with Dad to his yesteryears, spending time with him to write this book, I found an unexpected gift. Now, I know him before he was my dad. I know the boy who became a young man who became my father. Dad's old stories have more than one-liners; they have details. Now, old family photos have more than captions; they have whole stories.

I used to think my dad's past was ancient history. How could it have anything to do with me? But his history is my history. It shaped him and he shaped me. His loving ways helped me be a good mother and grandmother. That is his legacy, his greatest achievement as a father.

On top of that, knowing his history made history real for me. It isn't just events in books. The older I get the more I understand how the events of history are interwoven and not isolated, how we are all affected by events all over the world every day. I have a greater appreciation of my parents' and their comrades' contributions to their country, of the lives deflected by war.

One other note: From the day they got together after the war, my parents have rarely been apart. I realized early on that it would be impossible to write Dad's story without Mom's, so I strived to keep this in Dad's point of view. My mother, Emma L. Willey, wrote of her early life in *Prairie Rattlers, Long Johns and Chokecherry Wine* and her life with Dad in the sequel *Beyond the Silent Prairie* (PublishAmerica, 2003 and 2006).

1

Baby Boy

*1917: The U.S. declares war on Germany and
    enters World War I
Woodrow Wilson is president of the U.S.
Women suffragists picket the White House
One top song is "Huckleberry Finn"
Bread costs 9 cents a loaf, milk 44 cents a gallon,
    and a car can be purchased for $375*

"This is harder than a bull turd," said my dad one day
while trying to scoop ice cream from a carton. That's
Orman Willey for you. When he has to idle his red Buick at
a stop sign to wait for a long string of cars, I can bet on him
saying, "Who left the gate open?" Last summer when I
stayed in a motel with my parents for a family reunion, Dad
got out of bed one morning, tottered to the mirror, leaned in
to peer at his 90-year-old face, and said, "My eyes look like
two pee-holes in the snow."

You can take the cowboy from the ranch, but you can
never take the ranch from the cowboy.

***

I find myself wanting to stay longer now when I make the two-hour drive to visit my parents in Roseburg, Oregon. I want to hear more details in the stories my dad has always told about his cowboy days in South Dakota and his soldier years during World War II. I wonder if there are things that he would never have told a little girl, but could talk about now. Things he only told men? Perhaps he too realizes that he doesn't have forever, and he will reveal more now.

One day Dad and I, along with my mother, had lunch at Los Dos Amigos, one of their favorite restaurants. Afterwards inside their apartment, Dad opened the closet door and set his black cowboy-style hat in its place on the shelf. He wore a long-sleeved yoked shirt with snaps down the front and on its wide cuffs. His pants, though made of knit fabric, fit close with topstitching like jeans; and a trophy-style silver buckle closed his belt. He walked to his well-broken-in blue recliner, sank into it, and pulled the wood lever, which shot his legs out. Holding palms across his still-slim stomach, he said, "I'm fuller than a tick in hunting season."

Mom settled into her recliner. I kicked off my shoes and curled my feet under me on the couch. I expected to get to the bolder questions eventually, but that day, I started with something easy, keeping my notebook and pen within reach.

I asked Dad, "How do you break a horse?"

He grinned and said, "First, you have to catch him."

"Exactly how do you catch a wild horse?"

"You have to round up the whole herd and put them in the round corral."

"By yourself? Wouldn't they just run the other way or scatter when they saw you riding toward them?"

"Sometimes there would be a couple or three riders," Dad said. "And a good dog helps. If I was alone, sometimes I could get a bunch started in the direction of the section line. It had fences on both sides that would funnel them right into our corral."

"How many horses are you talking about?"

"Oh, ten to fifteen head. I'd pick out the one I wanted, a trim agile-looking one for a saddle horse. I'd rope him and then tie him to a snubbing post."

"Snubbing post?" I'd heard him use the term before, but now I wanted to know exactly what it was.

"A lone post inside the corral where we could tie a horse with a short rope. I'd open the gate and let the rest of the herd go back to the open range." He was always amazed that the lead mares always knew exactly where to go once the gate was opened. Cowboys never had to worry about wild horses finding their way back to the range.

I asked Dad to close his eyes and tell me what he smelled on those days.

"Horse shit," he said, without bothering to close his eyes. After Mom and I finished laughing, I asked what he heard.

"The stallion makes a sort of grunt while herding his mares, and the mares whinny to their colts." He slid his hand into his pants pocket and pulled out his pocketknife. Unfolding a blade, he cleaned and trimmed a fingernail.

"How did you learn to rope in the first place?"

"I watched my dad a lot." He snapped the knife blade closed and returned it to his pocket. "Some cowboys were very good and some not so good. I left that up to my dad as he was what I would call an expert. If he wasn't there, I had to do it myself, and it took me several attempts, but I usually got the job done. When we had time, we'd put a few calves in the corral and practice."

He added, "Before you can break a horse to ride, you've gotta break him to lead, and to do that, I'd tie him to a tame saddle horse and lead them both to a grassy area where the horses would be able to graze. We called this the stake line. We'd make it twenty or thirty feet long and tie it to something heavy like a mowing machine wheel. It would move, but only slightly, so the bronc wouldn't hurt himself if he ran to the end of the line. Every day I'd take feed to him and lead him to the creek for water. After three or four days on the stake line, the bronc could usually be lead to water with another saddle horse."

"He'd already gotten used to the bit and bridle?"

"That's right. By putting it on and taking it off many times. Then it was time to introduce him to the barn. And to the saddle. I'd put it on and take it off many times, until he was familiar with what was going on. Then I'd try to get on. You don't want to startle him, and you have to make sure he stands still while you are trying to mount."

"But how do you get him to stand still if he doesn't want to?"

Dad rubbed the back of his neck. "Just talk to him, pet him, and say whoa boy until he's still and try it again. When he'll let you stay on, it's time for the first ride. Snub him to a tame saddle horse with another rider, get on, and let the other horse lead him for a few miles. Then turn him loose and pray he doesn't buck. You're on your own now, just the cowboy and the bronc."

"Did it always work?"

"Usually, but we once led a bronc three miles and all the way back home, too, because he kept trying to buck. The secret is to keep 'em from bucking."

"But, how do you stop him?"

"You have to hold his head up. It wasn't easy, but you had to hold the reins or halter rope so tight he couldn't put his head down. If you could take his head away from him, it was a lot harder for him to buck. If he couldn't get his head between his legs, he'd sort of hop sideways, or crow hop, but he couldn't buck hard."

My mother, Emma Willey (nee Ruby), said, "Wild horses were trained to be workhorses, too, weren't they?" She grew up on a homestead called the Spring Creek Farm about thirty miles from the Willey place.

"Sure," said Dad. "We'd pick out the bigger heavier-set ones for that. We'd hitch them alongside another tame workhorse at first. They could work together to pull a plow, rake, cultivator, or manure spreader. Even a wagon or sled." He added that he would ride a newly-broken bronc at least twice a week driving cattle or whatever it had been taught to do. He said, "If you lost the stirrups, it was all over. I can still hear my dad hollering 'hold his head up' and 'lean back.'" He leaned back in his chair, as if on a horse, his body remembering the exact angle.

"So, I'm a cowboy's daughter, because you're a cowboy's son and grandson."

Dad's head came up, and his right hand ticked the air in front of him, as if in salute to his forebears. "I sure come by it honest."

His grandfather Curtis Willey moved by covered wagon from Iowa to the Dakota Territory in 1877. He brought along a string of Durham cattle that were cheaper and expected to do better than the more common Herefords that ranchers were raising in that area. He also brought his family that included toddler Absolum Day "Dode" Willey, my dad's dad.

This is the legend of how my Grandpa Willey got the nickname of Dode: When the family had just arrived in the Black Hills, he turned up missing one day. Everyone looked up and down the creek, but could find no trace of the little boy. Eventually, someone searched in an establishment of camp followers and entertainers known as "Across the Creek" and found the little boy sitting on a woman's lap. Her name was Dode, and the name stuck, perhaps for the simple reason that it was easier to say than Absolum.

By 1901 at age 26, Dode Willey was working for Sam Sheffield, the wagon boss at the Flying V cow outfit at Cedar Canyon on the Moreau River. In 1905 he filed on his own homestead in Perkins County near Date, South Dakota, and built a sod house in 1908 to replace the dugout he had been living in with a friend. Few trees grew in that arid landscape, so prairie homesteaders built homes out of bricks cut from sod. The prairies of northwestern South Dakota are not as expansive or flat as those of eastern South Dakota or Nebraska; they have more rolling hills, gullies, draws, and outcroppings of buttes, many large enough to have names like the Slim Buttes.

In 1910 at age 35, Dode married 18-year-old Clara Ellis from Kansas and moved her in a wagon the four miles from her parent's to his homestead. My sister-in-law Kate Willey says Clara once told her, "I was nervous on my wedding night, and Dode knew it, so when we stopped for the night, he pulled out a bottle of peppermint schnapps and gave me a drink right out of the bottle. That settled me down, and we spread our bedroll under the wagon. To this day I like a little schnapps." Some in the family doubt this story, including my dad and his sister Gladys. But my sister-in-law is good at that kind of conversation, and I can picture her and Grandma having an intimate little chat. Besides, I hope it happened, and I like to imagine Grandma fighting a smile and a blush as she talked about it.

Clara's new home, nestled less than a quarter of a mile from Rabbit Creek, consisted solely of the sod house. Her closest neighbor lived half a mile away, while the closest town was Strool, twelve miles to the northwest as the crow flies. Grandma said (recorded when her middle-aged sons asked her to talk about the old days): "I didn't have much when I moved in, believe me! I could just about take all my clothes in a bandanna handkerchief. When I went to keepin' house, we had an old cook stove, a homemade table, two homemade chairs, and an old iron bed. My cupboards I made from orange crates and I put little curtains to them, that was my cupboards. My dresser was orange crates, too. The walls weren't plastered, and the roof was boards, then tar paper, then sod to hold the tar paper down."

While Clara "went to housekeeping," Dode took care of their place, but also hired out to others. While wagon boss at the L7 Ranch in about 1912, he helped five other cowboys bring in over six hundred head of cattle, crossing the Missouri River on a pontoon bridge at Evarts, South Dakota. He also worked for the DZ outfit on the Standing Rock Indian Reservation and in 1913 moved to Fort Yates, North Dakota, to help winter 1,800 steers. His family lived in a log cabin, where they were burned out when an oil lamp fell to the floor while Clara was moving a table it sat on. According to his obituary in the *Bison Courier*, Dode also "ran the first county road outfit in Perkins County and worked on the railroad at Lemmon and the government corral at Belle Fourche."

Dode returned to the Rabbit Creek homestead once or twice a month, often enough that Clara delivered four children in the first four years of her marriage: Robert Curtis "R.C" (1910), Bonnie Marguerite (1911), Gladys Marcelle (1912), and Noble Day (1914).

Orman Othe Willey

Clara gave birth to my dad, Orman Othe Willey on August 23, 1917, in Hettinger, North Dakota, about thirty miles from the homestead. The family had moved there so Dode could take a job delivering mail by car to Strool, South Dakota. They returned to the homestead later, where the sixth and last child, Alden Ellis, was born in 1921. However, I never heard Dad or his siblings call Alden anything but Aldy or Babe.

I have always wondered how Grandma Willey came up with the unusual names for her sons. In her later years, she joked that she named her youngest Alden for All Done. In an old family picture I found an uncle named Othe, so that probably explains Dad's middle name. And, because our family went fishing at Orman Dam when I was a kid, I wondered if that was the source of Dad's first name. Dad didn't know, so I asked his older sister Gladys, who verified my theory. Orman Dam was built near Belle Fourche as an irrigation project in 1905 and completed in 1917, the year Dad was born. As a kid, I thought the place was named after my dad. At the time it was finished, it was the largest earthen dam in the world, and hundreds of local farmers used their own teams and equipment to help build it.

Dad's earliest memory as a toddler, or as he said, "before I could pee hard against the ground," is of waking in the night from a bad dream. He doesn't remember what it was about, but said, "Mother came in and held me." He and his brothers Noble and Aldy shared one bedroom in the back of the house. After Clara had been on the homestead awhile, Dode used a flatbed wagon and team of horses to move in a frame house, which he set next to the sod house to accommodate his growing family. A porch was added later. Outbuildings appeared gradually: two barns, a garage, and a granary. They used a bucket on a rope to get water from a well in the yard and stored food down in the well. Dad said, "I can still taste the cold milk out of that well."

When talking about that house in the old tape recording, Grandma said, "We went to many a dance when we lived there, I'll tell you."

I asked Dad how people knew about dances, since they didn't have telephones in Perkins County until about 1934.

"Oh, they'd just tell someone they ran into," said Dad. "Maybe a neighbor, and the word spread. Someone would bring a fiddle, and pretty soon toes were tapping."

Mom piped up from her recliner. "Didn't your dad call square dances?"

"He sure did. And the men usually had a bottle of moonshine to pass around outside."

The Willeys knew how to have fun, but got the work done, too. From an early age, everyone in the family helped. When Dad was little, early one morning he went to the barn to get milk in his thick white porcelain cup.

Noble, his older brother by three years, was milking the cows and said to Dad, "What makes you think you can have any milk? You didn't help with the milking, did you?"

Dad hit Noble in the head with his thick white ceramic cup, breaking the cup into many pieces. He said, "But Noble got his way and from that day on, I had to help with the milking."

I could imagine my grandmother Clara trying to sweep the floor or bake bread, bumping into children at every turn. I asked Dad how she handled it.

He said, "Ma just shooed us out the door and told us to 'Go on out and get the stink blowed off.' Especially when the weather was nice."

Dad played in the sand on the banks of Rabbit Creek, scooping it into little piles to make hills for make-believe cars. They might have been matchboxes or blocks of wood, anything that would make trails in the sand. He spent a lot of time making his own toys, even his own little tractor out of pieces of metal and part of an old horse-drawn mowing machine. To play ball, he and his brothers and friends dug turtle eggs out of the sand hills by the creek, and an inflated pig's bladder worked pretty well for a football. He made his own bow and arrows out of willow branches, and arrowheads out of scrap iron he found on the top of an old wagon box. He'll never forget the first jackrabbit he shot with an arrow; it was sitting under a Russian thistle, also known as a tumbleweed, not ten feet away. His face looking boyish, he said, "It was an easy shot."

I asked if he took it home for his mother to cook.

"Oh no," he said. "We never cooked jackrabbits. They

always seemed to have sores on them or worms."

Mom said, "Our family didn't eat jackrabbits either. We ate mostly canned meat in winter, but if my brothers brought home cottontails, we enjoyed the chance for fresh meat."

Dad nodded. All his life, he heard the story, told "a hundred times" by his mother, about the time when he was four or five years old and embarrassed everyone, including company, at the supper table. When his stomach growled, little Orman brightened and proudly announced, "There, my bowels moved."

He loved his boyhood dog named Ring, a black and white collie that went everywhere with him. With Ring by their side, he and his brothers and friends fished in Rabbit Creek for bullheads and suckers. They made poles from willow switches from the trees along the bank and used worms and bacon fat for bait. They often swam in the creek during hot summers and picked chokecherries and buffalo berries nearby. Unfortunately, when he got older, Ring had to be put down, because my grandpa Dode became afraid he would hurt someone. Dad said, "Ring got so he'd snap at a neighbor kid if he tagged me or my brothers or sisters in a game of Pump Pump Pull Away."

Among the horses around the Willey homestead, there was usually a kid-friendly one. Dad fondly remembers a bay with one white spot on his right front leg. "Monk was so gentle," Dad said, "we could walk between his legs or under his belly. When the folks turned me loose on him, I must've ridden a thousand miles up and down Rabbit Creek."

As the third son, Dad seldom got new clothes, but when he was about six years old, he got a new gray-blue wool coat for Christmas. While out playing Hide and Seek, he got hot, took off his coat and hung it on the fence of the pigpen. When the game was done and he went after his coat, the old sow had pulled it into the pen and ripped it to pieces. He said, "I knew I had to tell Mother and went bawling to the house."

His mother looked sad, but let him off easy and said only, "Well, what did you hang it on the fence for?"

She once made Dad wear his sister Gladys's black oxford shoes to the Christmas program at school, because he didn't have any decent ones. Dad said, "I wished I could stay home, but then I thought of the candy or new pencils with my name on them that Santa Claus might hand out." It turned out that no one noticed his footwear after all.

Clara didn't spank often, but would resort to a single swat on the seat of his pants now and then to make her point. Dode once delivered a painful spanking with a willow stick after my dad and a friend went into a neighbor's house while they were gone and helped themselves to food. Dad said, "John and I were out riding one day looking for wild berries. When we came by the Harben place, we decided to stop to see Stella as she was a great cook. She wasn't home, but had left just-baked bread and donuts on the table. We helped ourselves and knew better, too, but they looked so tempting."

In the days long before political correctness, Dode always said it was time to mow hay, "when the grass was ass-deep to an Indian." Once when Dad was supposed to be mowing, he got sleepy, brought the team to a halt, and lay down in the shade of one of the horses for a quick snooze. He said, "I woke up to the noise of the mowing machine and thought the team had started to run away." He jumped up to stop them and found his dad driving them. It always impressed him that his dad never said a word and just commenced with the mowing that day. "A spanking wouldn't have hurt as bad as letting my Dad down on a job he sent me out to do."

I asked why he didn't get run over by the mower, and Dad explained that he had lain down on the left side of the horse, while the mower followed directly behind the horses and the scythe fell to the right of the mower.

To this day, if you are searching for something and find it close by, especially if it was there all the time, my dad will say with glee, "If it was a snake it would've bit you!" If you lived in the arid land of northwestern South Dakota, you heard plenty about rattlesnakes, and you respected them, because people could die from their venom. My mother remembers the rattles whacked from the tail ends of snakes killed around the Ruby place. She said, "I can still see them in that jar sitting on the windowsill in the pantry."

Dad has a rattlesnake story to top that one.

2

School Boy

1920: Prohibition begins
1924: A Ford can be purchased for $299
1927: Charles Lindbergh flies solo across the
Atlantic
Mount Rushmore monument is dedicated
Babe Ruth hits sixty home runs
1928: Herbert Hoover is elected president and "I
Faw Down an' Go Boom" is a hit song
1929: The Stock market crashes and nine months
later the Great Depression begins

In 1928, when Dad was eleven years old, relatives named the Wildes arrived for a visit. Early on the first morning, my dad's parents Dode and Clara sat around the breakfast table with their company. But Dad and his cousin Curtis finished breakfast as fast as they could, having been given permission to go grouse hunting. They excused themselves and struck out across the rolling prairie, Clara warning, "Now you boys, watch out for rattlesnakes!"

However, an excited boy with his city cousin in tow can get distracted. About a quarter mile from the house Dad stepped on a rattlesnake. Living up to its reputation, the snake darted out of the grass and sank its fangs into my dad's lower right leg. As for what happened next, Dad said, "After kicking the snake loose from my pants, I did the worst thing possible, jumped the creek and ran for home. Figured I was good as dead."

When he slammed into the house, he found his mother and seventeen-year-old sister Bonnie doing dishes.

Clara said, "Bonnie, go out and catch a couple chickens and slap them on that bite." She believed the raw meat would act like a warm poultice and draw out the venom.

Bonnie ran outside, chased squawking chickens around the dusty yard until she caught one, tore it open, and one after the other pressed chicken onto the snakebite. In telling the story later, she always said, "The chicken came off green."

Clara ran to get the aging Model T, and Bonnie helped Dad climb in. Clara sped two miles to a group of men working on a road, hoping to find someone to cut the wound, the custom in those days. If she did it herself, she feared she would cut too deeply, and her son would bleed to death. However, when she got to the road crew, a group of men gathered and just stood around debating what to do next. Someone handed my dad a pint of whiskey and told him to drink it.

I asked Dad if he drank any.

"Well," he said, "I don't remember exactly how much I drank, but the stories I heard later always went, 'The kid drank a whole pint of whiskey and that's what saved his life.'"

One man had a razor and said he would cut the bite, but he backed out, afraid he didn't know how. Someone else suggested they tie a tourniquet above the bite and drive on to Hettinger, North Dakota, to see Doc Schumacher. It would be about thirty miles, so Mr. O'Leary from the road crew offered to drive them in his more reliable newer car. On the way they picked up my grandpa Dode Willey at a ranch where he was working. By the time Dad, his parents, and Mr. O'Leary got to Hettinger, the tourniquet was nearly out of sight because of swelling. Dad said, "By then the whiskey was doing its job."

"What do you mean?" I asked.

"Taking away the fear of dying!"

Doc Schumacher removed the tourniquet and insisted that Dad's leg be lanced four times two inches above the bite. Dad said, "That hurt like the dickens, and it took both Dad and Mr. O'Leary to hold me down." Afterwards, Doc washed up, saying, "Now you're all fixed up." Dad liked the sound of that and took it to mean he wouldn't die.

His parents had to get back to the ranch, but left him in Hettinger to recuperate for about ten days in a big old house by the railroad tracks, in the care of "a kind old lady." He enjoyed watching and listening to the trains that whistled through town several times a day and night, describing it as, "quite a novelty for a country boy." His parents came to see him several times, and he said, "I wish I could remember that lady's name as she sure did take wonderful care of me. She even wheeled me in a wheelchair down town a few times." He went home with a pair of crutches that he used for a couple of months.

After the snakebite healed, the scar looked like a bear claw track, and it still does. Sometimes it "acts up," as Dad calls it, and he will reach down and rub or scratch it. After you hear the snakebite story, he might tell you about the time years later when he escaped death from an accidental shooting during hunting season. He might even let you feel

BBs that remain under the skin of his right arm. They have been there for over fifty years.

Dode, Clara, Bonnie, R.C., Gladys, Noble, Orman, and Aldy "Babe" in 1925

Long before the snakebite incident when my dad was seven or eight years old, he and his friend Eddie Fuller wanted to go camping. But their mothers thought they were too young and wouldn't give them the go-ahead until they agreed not to stay out overnight. The boys planned for an all-day outing and packed bread, pork and beans, and potatoes for the noon meal. Dad said, "The highlight of the episode was the bonfire to cook our food. Needless to say, we burned it all, not knowing how to regulate the fire. But we ate it anyway." He added, "To this day I could walk right to the spot we had that campout." They spent the rest of the day digging a hole in the ground at the top of a knoll, planning to return later and put a roof over their hideout, but never did.

When my dad was about ten years old, his dad ordered a new shotgun for him from the Montgomery Ward catalog, paying seven dollars for it. But because his dad was away from home working so much, an old bachelor who lived in the area taught him how to shoot when he grew old enough to hunt. My dad said, "Old Dad Newberry always said he could pound a nail into a clothesline post and drive it on in with a bullet, but I never saw the proof of that or talked to anyone who did."

Whenever Dad and his brothers had free time, they fired away at cottontails, grouse or muskrats. They found they could flood some critters out of their holes, and then Patsy, their rat terrier, took over for the kill. "If Patsy saw them," said Dad, "they were a goner." The county, when presented with proof at the courthouse in Bison, paid ten-cent bounties for gopher tails. The boys once tried to make two tails out of one long one, but Dad said, "We got caught and that was the end of trying to cheat." Magpie heads brought ten-cent bounties, too, because the large black and white birds of the crow family damaged field crops, robbed other birds' nests and ate their eggs, and even pecked newborn sheep or calves to death.

The family didn't travel the twenty miles to town often, but when the boys had money, they usually bought ammunition for their guns. "Then of course," said Dad, "we liked a Baby Ruth or Bit-O-Honey candy bar or an ice cream cone when they were available."

Freezing winter temperatures meant Rabbit Creek could be skated on. Snowfall and blizzards made banks and drifts for sledding, and the long sloping hills around the place had Dad and his brothers and pals making skis and sleds. They used steam to curve boards into skis, strapped them on, and sometimes recruited a horse to pull them. In one mishap with the sled, Dad missed the gate and went through a barbed wire fence. "My clothes looked like they went through a threshing machine."

"What about you?" I had to ask, knowing first-hand how vicious barbed wire can be to a fast-moving kid. I still have a long scar on the back of my leg.

Dad said, "I had cuts on my arms and legs and some on my belly, but none on my face. Just darned lucky!"

To make extra spending money all winter long, Dad trapped muskrats, mink and weasels. In the gray-dim dawn, he bundled up in coat, hat, and gloves and headed for Rabbit Creek. "I used to run my trap line on skates, and it wasn't too uncommon to skate a mile in each direction from the ranch. My brothers and I thought we were doing real well if we got two animals a night." Old Doc Newberry showed the boys how to tack the furs to stretcher boards for several days of drying before mailing to furriers.

In winter there were fewer chores and more time for family fun. At home in the evenings, they might make popcorn or fudge and play Whist, Cribbage or Rummy. Dad's sister Bonnie wrote in a family memory book by my mother Emma Willey titled *Willey Family History*, about Dode sitting in an old rocking chair next to the pot-bellied stove with two children on his lap and others standing behind him, everyone singing songs. She also described how her little brothers continually wore out the knees of their overalls by pretending to be horses with jar rings cupped in their hands to make the clopping of horse hooves.

The family might join neighbors at their house for card parties, where the preferred game was Pitch. Dad said, "Mr. Tescher, we called him Tesh, made oyster stew in a big copper boiler and let it simmer while they played. I can almost smell it now."

I asked where they got the oysters. Mom said,

"Probably used canned oysters from the store, but sometimes fresh ones were shipped to Hettinger by railroad."

"You're not talking about prairie oysters, are you?" I asked, knowing that was what they called the fried testicles of calves. My parents tried serving them, as well as brains, to me as a kid, but even though they tasted good, once I found out what they were, I said, "No, thanks."

Dad's face brightened. "We had those at branding time every year," he said. "We dehorned and castrated the calves and cooked the oysters on a stick in the fire that kept the branding irons hot." By the look on his face, he would happily do it again, given the opportunity.

On winter nights, it often grew too cold to walk the hundred feet or so to the outhouse, so the family kept a can in the house. My dad still uses the expression "going to the can" for bathroom visits. Taking the can to the outhouse each morning always sparked fierce debate about whose turn it was.

Summertime chores kept all hands busy until dark. Dad had to help his mother with her vegetable garden, hoeing weeds, hauling water from the creek, and sometimes hand picking potato bugs from plants and dropping them into buckets of kerosene. He hated those garden tasks, but said, "On the brighter side, I always enjoyed the fresh things. The melons were small, but we grew quite a few, and they were sweet and juicy." No wonder my parents greet ear corn season to this day with glee. When they were kids, they plucked ears from the stalks, cooked them, smeared them with homemade butter, and ate them. Now, that's fresh corn.

Another food memory for Dad was the time he went over to the neighbors to play, and his friend dug out a five gallon bucket of honey to make sandwiches. When the friend took the lid off the can, "thousands of flies" buzzed out, but he made them each a sandwich anyway.

About once a year, the well had to be cleaned out. "Oh I hated that job!" Dad said. If a mouse or something got into the well and died, they could taste it, and that's what usually prompted a cleaning. Dad or one of his brothers had to stand in a bucket and be let down into the well, where he stood in cold water about two feet deep and groped around for the dead animal. Other times they had to scoop sand and gravel out of the well.

The Willey boys were expected to haul wood, carry water, and feed hogs, and as Dad put it, "We were always expected to pick up the traces when Dad was gone." The traces are the lines of the harness that attach an animal or team to a wagon. The boys learned not to cuss or fart around the house, because if Dode heard them, he always said, "If you're going to do that, go out to the barn."

When the boys grew older, after working hard all week, on Saturday night they were free to go to town for some fun; in Bison, Strool, or Reva they saw friends, played pool or went to a dance. Sometimes their dad gave them two bits spending money. When I was a kid, I heard Grandpa Dode use the words "two bits" and asked my dad how much money it was. He said it was a quarter.

***

Each September brought the beginning of a new school year. On weekday mornings Dad left for grade school about 8:30 in the morning. No matter the weather he always walked about a mile across the prairie or a mile and a quarter by road to a schoolhouse with eight grades in one room. Before he left, the family gathered around the table for breakfast, Dode and Clara on the ends, kids on benches along the sides. Clara often made oatmeal and toasted homemade bread. Sometimes she fixed bacon and eggs or quite often, pancakes. "We also had baking powder biscuits, which Mother made the best in the world, my favorite," said Dad, grinning. Even now, at home or in a restaurant, when Dad splits a hot biscuit, butters it and slathers it with honey, I see the face of the boy who loved his mother's biscuits.

For lunch on school days, Dad's mother packed his lunch in a five-pound bucket that lard or peanut butter came in, writing his name on it. She made sandwiches with leftover boiled beans or home-canned beef, but peanut butter and jelly were my dad's favorite. He is still fond of peanut butter, and if I forget to put it on the table when he visits, he will say, "Say, do you have any peanut butter?" His mother also packed canned fruit in a jar and cookies or cake for dessert. Dad got home from school about 4:30 in the afternoon, and usually had chores to do before play.

I asked if he liked school.

"Oh yes," he said. "Sure did."

"Were you a good student?"

"Well, I wouldn't say that," he said. "Now you've put me on the spot."

"I think he liked recess," said Mom, teasing.

Dad said, "I did like to find a garter snake, curl it up in my hand and get one of the girls to come over and see what I had to show them."

Sometimes Dad and his friend John Tish got in trouble for the Halloween tricks they dreamed up. Once they rode over to a mean neighbor's place and took a few turkeys off the hayrack where they had roosted for the night and threw them into the neighbor's new car. Dad said, "The old man shot at us, but on the way out, we opened the gate and turned his bucks in with the ewes."

I had to ask. "He shot at two boys?"

"I suppose he shot in the air to scare us, but we were too far away anyway for him to hit us."

Another time while out riding horses when they were about fourteen, Dad and John found something so unusual, they had to stop and investigate. "While crossing a little hill along a bank," Dad said, "the ground under the horses' hooves sounded hollow. We turned around and went back over it again. Still didn't sound right, so we got off our horses to look around." It turned out to be a cave built into the bank, a whiskey still or cache as some called it. They found six barrels of mash brewing, plus all the equipment to run off the whiskey. This was about 1931, and Prohibition was not repealed until 1933.

When Dad got home, he reported the cache to his brothers, who later told a couple of their friends. Someone said, "Let's run her off," and a few days later R.C., Noble, Dad and a couple other friends returned to the scene of discovery. After tasting the whiskey, they packed it out in a five-gallon can, poured it into smaller containers, and stashed it up and down the creek for later. Noble said to Dad years later, "We had our big problem, finding containers, didn't we? We cleaned Mom out of quart jars, gallon jugs, anything that would hold liquid." Their parents were gone at the time, probably to the Black Hills or Iowa to visit relatives. The boys figured the still belonged to a neighbor. Dad said, "Some of it must have floated into the Missouri River."

***

There were no high schools close enough to walk to, so after graduation from the eighth grade in Perkins County, special arrangements had to be made for further education. For ninth grade, Dode and Clara arranged for my dad to stay in Strool with his Aunt Dell and Uncle Charlie Ellis, Clara's brother. Dad doesn't remember for sure, but in all likelihood, Dode and Clara traded farm fresh eggs and milk for Dad and his horse's room and board. He and his cousin Marjorie rode six miles on horseback to the high school in a town called Cash, and Dad often rode his horse home on weekends.

It was about this time that he remembers how proud he was to graduate from denim overalls to his first pair of pants to wear with a belt like his dad's. He guesses they came from a Sears and Roebuck catalog, but his mother sewed most of his long-sleeve button-down shirts.

Another vivid memory from ninth grade was the day he and his friends were throwing snowballs at each other during recess, and the teacher stuck her head out of the window at the same moment Dad made a pitch. He said, "I hit her right in the face with a snowball, and she made me stand in the corner and rub my nose on the plaster wall."

While he lived with his Aunt Dell, she impressed on Dad how important it was to continue his education. Also that year, a good friend of his mother's, a teacher named Francena Schar, told him about the Agriculture High School in Brookings known as Aggie. It had a program with nine months of vocational agriculture classes compressed into five months to give rural students more time to work on their parents' farms and ranches and still go to school.

Dad liked the sound of that, so when he got home that summer he told his parents he wanted to go to Aggie. He spent the summer working around the home place for his dad, herded sheep for the Holtrys, and hired out to a neighbor named Ira Berge down on the Moreau River, where he cut wood and milked cows for "not much money, but I was glad to get it."

In the meantime, Clara wrote to the agriculture college to find out how much the high school program would cost. Brookings was on the other side of the state, so not only would Aggie require tuition, but room and board for five months and travel expenses to get there. By this time, the Depression was setting in, and Dode was finding it hard to pay taxes on the homestead. That left no money for Aggie.

Dad had to settle for another option. For his second year of high school, he left the rolling prairie, gullies and arid buttes of Perkins County for Sturgis, population 1,700, where he stayed with his sister Bonnie and her husband Russell Steeves, who worked at his parents' dairy. Though less than a hundred miles south of home, the Black Hills offered granite mountains, pine tree forests, clear blue streams and lakes.

At Sturgis High School, Dad studied algebra, world history, English, and geography, and played on the football team. His sister Gladys lived in Sturgis then, too, and owned the Cozy Café on the south side of Main Street. She hired Dad to wash dishes, and he walked to Fort Meade, an Army post two miles east of town, to earn a dollar a day washing dishes for F Troop.

A few times he hitchhiked home, once catching a ride with a guy who made moonshine whiskey. "He had two fifteen-gallon kegs in his truck," Dad said. "We boosted the kegs up to the attic of a house in Sturgis. Then I jumped into the attic and rolled them to the rear and out of sight. They were pretty heavy, but I could roll them."

While Dad was away at school, the homestead was lost to someone who paid the back taxes. Dode hired on as ranch manager for Andy Thybo, and he, Clara, and Aldy, the only child still living at home, moved into a house on Thybo's Arrowhead Ranch. For the first time, Clara had a washing machine, and though her house was still made of sod, she was pleased it didn't look like it, because it was stuccoed.

A few months after starting the tenth grade in Sturgis, Dad dropped out. When I asked why, a sad look overtook his face. He said, "That just wasn't for me. I was homesick, and I wanted to work and save money for Aggie." So, he moved back home with his parents and went to work for Andy Thybo, which meant he worked for his dad. At the age of fifteen, Orman Willey became a cowboy. He earned a dollar a day.

3

Cowboy

*1935: Franklin D. Roosevelt is president
Hitler orders German radio stations not to play
    music by blacks or Jews
The game of Monopoly is introduced by Parker
    Brothers
Best Picture at the Academy Awards is* Mutiny on
the Bounty
*A top song is "This Time It's Love" by Sam
    Lewis
Bread costs 8 cents a loaf and milk 47 cents a
    gallon
Average income is $1,594 per year*

In the years before fences enclosed ranches on the Great Plains, herds of wild horses roamed the wide-open spaces. Dode Willey, Orman Willey's father, was one of many cattlemen who built his herd of horses by helping himself to wild ones and breaking them to saddle or harness. After saying goodbye to high school in Sturgis, my dad eagerly reported for his new job with his dad at the Arrowhead Ranch. Owner Andy Thybo told his new man he would pay ten dollars for every wild horse broken. Dad especially looked forward to working with horses again, but every ranch hand was expected to help with everything from fixing fences to branding, roundups and preparation of fields for raising grain and corn for winter feed.

One morning, Dode figured the cowboys needed a new saddle horse, so my dad saddled a big sorrel named Silver and rode out to find the wild bunch. A few hours later he had rounded up about twenty head and run them home to the round corral.

"As I watched them mill around," he said, "one kept taking my eye. All black except for white feet. Spookier than the rest, and his white eyes danced as he ran circles trying to escape. I picked him and named him White Eye, but let me tell you he was a challenge for this cowboy." He shook his head. "That horse was so unpredictable. Sometimes I went to the barn to get him, and he acted just like any other horse, but other times he acted like he'd never seen a human being before."

Dode reminded his son that sometimes a daylong ride would help tame a horse. So, after Dad had been working with White Eye for a while, he rode him over to neighbor Ike John's place one morning, where he found his brother R.C. and a guy named Harold Coe drinking coffee. Dad tied White Eye to the fence and joined the men for a chat.

When he was ready to leave, he got on White Eye, but the horse got his head down and started to buck. Dad said, "I stayed on but lost the reins, and that horse bucked all the way to the road ditch, across the road, and out into a field. Thank God he stopped at the fence. I was afraid he would go on through it."

I asked if the other fellows made smart remarks or

laughed.

"No," he said. "They smiled and hollered things I should try, but I was so embarrassed I lost control. Especially in front of Harold. He rode in rodeos, you know."

"You didn't want to look like a greenhorn in front of an old pro."

"Course not."

"But you didn't get bucked off?"

"No, I leaned forward in the saddle and petted White Eye on the shoulder and talked to him until I could reach the reins. Then he took me all the way home without stopping."

When Dode decided White Eye looked ready for a longer training ride, he suggested that his son ride him to the Slim Buttes to pick up a bull. Clara made it clear she was not happy that her son would be spending the day on the wild bronco she had heard plenty about. She worried until after dark that night, but her son finally rode in on White Eye, reporting that the horse had done all that was asked of him.

My dad often heard his dad singing "The Strawberry Roan" out on the range, so I imagine he did, too, riding through the Slim Buttes on White Eye, a smile on his face, hardly believing his luck that someone would pay him to ride a horse.

Besides the Slim Buttes in that area, you can find Adam and Eve, Dears Ears, Bear Butte, and Ghost Butte. I wondered if my dad ever thought about the history of the Slim Buttes area when he rode there, but he says, no, he never heard much about that. In 1874, about fifty years before my dad's time, Lt. Col. George Armstrong Custer likely rode through the Slim Buttes on his way to the Black Hills from Fort Abraham Lincoln near Bismark, North

Dakota. It is easy to see how he, leading over a thousand men, would be attracted by green trees, springs, and creeks after crossing vast prairies on his way to explore the Black Hills for the U. S. government. Two years later in 1876, General George Crook dealt the Sioux a major setback in the same area as they fought to keep the Black Hills during the Indian Wars.

My dad always told another story about wild horses. One morning he saddled a black mare named Babe and rode out to find the wild bunch. "Babe was loping along at a brisk pace, when suddenly she came to a ditch, planted her front feet and slid to a stop. I kept on going of course, right over her head, and lit on my hands." That was the end of searching for wild horses that day, but he managed to climb back on Babe and ride her home. His mother took him to Doc Lister, who lived on a nearby ranch, and diagnosed a broken wrist that probably hampered the cowboy style for a while.

While working for Andy Thybo, Dad once got sent to work on another ranch Thybo owned called the T-Diamond Bar. Dad, with a grim look to his face, referred to the place as the Rock Ranch. Andy sent him out with a team of horses and a lumber wagon with a specially-rigged box to collect as-big-as-he-could-carry hunks of quartz and petrified wood to be used for new building foundations. Dad drove the wagon around the Slim Buttes, hunted for and loaded up rocks until he had the wagon full and hauled them back to the ranch. He said, "Then I had to unload them all," in a tone suggesting that wrangling rocks was nowhere near the fun of wrangling horses.

Andy sent him to his next assignment at the Bar-H Ranch in the Slim Buttes, owned and operated by his son Jim. The land was so dry that year that some cattle had to be summered elsewhere or sold at low prices. The Thybos planned to move a large herd and began gathering them from about a sixty square mile area. When the cattle were ready, Dad helped trail them to the railhead at Fruitdale (near Belle Fourche). He said, "Me and three other cowboys and a cook with a chuck wagon trailed over a thousand head a hundred and fifty miles."

But before he left, knowing he would be gone awhile, he went home to see his folks and tell them goodbye. He left early one morning riding Silver and leading White Eye, so he'd have two saddle horses on the drive. He said, "I'll never forget riding up over the divide and coming upon all those cattle. I usually rode in back, with a rider on each side and Andy in front. I could often see the whole bunch while moving down through a valley." No doubt on nice days a clear sky showcased puffy white clouds, for the big blue sky that Montana is famous for does not stop at the state line.

The trail cook rarely helped to wrangle cows, but usually went ahead with the mess wagon. He had enough to do with cooking and scouting ahead for campsites for the cowboys as well as the cattle. The first night they camped at the Vrooman ranch, a nice day's distance to ride. Not ready to trust White Eye to stake him out in the open, Dad put his horses in the round corral where there was hay to eat. He unrolled his bedroll outside the corral and settled down to sleep.

The next morning he planned to ride White Eye, but when he took him out of the corral, "the son-of-a-gun decided to buck. But I contained him, and that was the last time he ever bucked with me. Before that he kind of had me buffaloed, because I was a little afraid of him and he knew it. But finally during that long trail ride I got that sucker trained."

The second night they camped south of the Slim Buttes

near Sheep Mountain at the head of the Moreau River. As they did every night, they hobbled the horses (tied them together loosely) and each cowboy took his turn as night guard to watch the horses and keep the cattle together.

Dad said, "Sometimes I had to roll out my bedroll after dark. That night I heard an occasional rattle close by when the cattle moved around and I realized I had bedded down close to a den of rattlesnakes."

"That must have been scary after being bitten by one," I said. "What did you do?"

"Just laid there real still and hoped none of them came any closer."

I imagined a campfire flickering and conversation hopping from bedroll to bedroll, while the rest of the cowboys swapped legends about rattlesnakes.

Dad closed the subject with, "Andy always said there was an old saying that if a cowboy laid his rope in a circle around his bedroll, a snake wouldn't go over it. But I never saw anybody try it."

On that trip, one of the two green broncs that had only been halter-broken when the ride began dumped my dad early one frosty morning. He said, "It was the hardest I was ever thrown from a bucking horse." But he didn't dare swear. The cowboy life could include "chapping," a custom he'd heard about from his dad and other older cowboys. Anyone who used bad language, cheated, lied, or complained, especially about the food, could be made to walk between a gauntlet of cowboys. They would take off their chaps and slap at the offender's behind as he moved between them, and a cowboy could be sent packing if the violation was considered serious enough.

When the cowboys arrived at Fruitdale, they loaded the cattle onto a train and got on the train with them, because there would be more trailing to do at the destination. The train headed south through Hot Springs and on into Nebraska at Chadron, where it veered east toward Cody and Valentine. When the train got to Cody, the cowboys got off with their herd and drove it north about ten miles into South Dakota to the Rosebud Indian Reservation. Dad stayed with the cattle for two weeks, but then his boss sent him back to the ranch with nine head of saddle horses. He loaded them onto the train and rode the boxcar. Near Sturgis he got off the train to visit his sister Gladys.

Early the next morning he hitchhiked to Fruitdale to catch up with the horses and the train. After unloading the horses, still about eighty miles from home, he stopped for the night at Noble and Florence Rose's place, relatives of his parents.

"The next morning," Dad said, "I got up before daylight and by about seven that night I'd trailed the horses back to the Bar-H in the Slim Buttes. I took care of the horses, cleaned myself up, and went to a dance in Reva that night." He shook his head in wonder, and a smile tugged at the corners of his mouth. "Hadn't had enough riding and rode six miles to the dance."

Oh, how I would love to step back in time and see that handsome young cowboy strut into the dance hall, ready with tales of his trail ride.

Dad always kept his eye out for wild horses on the range. One day he realized he hadn't seen one bunch for over a week and rode out to look for them. He said, "I had ridden all day. I was hungry because I didn't take lunch along. Hadn't planned to be out all day. I was riding up a deep little ravine, when my horse came to a dead stop, his ears straight up and forward. I tried to spur him on, but he wouldn't budge." Soon, he found out why. A few yards away lay a bloated dead horse—the stud horse that had been running with that wild bunch. Dad found another dead horse a short distance up the hill, moved closer to take a look, and saw seven more dead horses in a pile on top of the hill. He assumed lightning had killed them.

I asked how he could tell.

"When it's storming, a bunch of horses will run to a high point and get real close together, and that's why a bolt of lightning could get them all at once. They'll bunch up like that to protect themselves from flies, too."

About five days later, while riding near the same area, he found a lone colt and assumed it was a survivor of the lightning episode. He said, "I figured the little one survived because he was off running the way a colt will do." He took him home, raised him, and eventually broke him for a saddle horse.

I thought that must have been a very special horse to him. "What did you name him?"

Dad puzzled for several moments and finally said with sadness in his eyes, "You know, I just don't remember."

I've never seen pictures of Dad as a cowboy. I don't know if any were taken, and besides, all of Dode and Clara's and my parents' family photos were destroyed in a house fire in 1947. I asked him what he wore during his cowboy years. He said jeans, plaid long-sleeve shirts, work shoes, and cowboy hats that were "smaller-rimmed then." He mail-ordered his first pair of cowboy boots from Justin Boots. He said the rich cowboys wore Stetson hats rated with stars in the catalog, from one to three or maybe four. He said with pride, "I had a three-star one once."

I said, "Except for the Rock Ranch, it sounds like you really enjoyed the cowboy years. Did you ever think about giving up the plan to go to Aggie?"

"Never. I kept giving my pay to Mother for safekeeping. I found out about a new way to make money, too."

4

College Boy

*1939: In September, France and Great Britain
    declare war on Germany*
*Pan Am begins first regularly scheduled
    transatlantic air service*
Scientists split the atom
World's Fair is held in New York
Movie tickets cost 22 cents
Gone With the Wind *is released at the movie
    theaters*
The number one song is "Deep Purple"

To boost his savings for Aggie, the agricultural high school in Brookings, Orman Willey signed up for the Civilian Conservation Corps (CCCs). During the Great Depression, the federal government established the Corps to provide jobs for half a million young men across America. In South Dakota alone at least thirty military-style camps were set up with, beds, tools, vehicles and even dishes left over from World War I. At first enrollees earned thirty dollars a month, twenty-five of which they agreed to send home to their families. For perspective, the average annual income in the U.S. was $1,900 a year, or less than $160 a month.

While reading about the CCC history, I was amazed at the speed at which the program was instituted—it took only thirty-seven days from the day of Franklin D. Roosevelt's inauguration until the first enrollee was inducted. This made me curious about how the word got out, so I asked my dad how he found out about it.

"I suppose," he said, "Mother or Aunt Dell read about it in the paper and told me."

Dad thought it over and decided to trade cowboy boots for work boots and enlisted. Assigned to Camp Oreville southwest of Hill City, he enjoyed living in the Black Hills again, where he hadn't spent much time since going to high school in Sturgis. He and his fellow recruits built roads and parks and got an education in forestry. Besides barracks and mess halls, CCC camps had ball fields, gyms and nearby lakes and streams for fishing and swimming on days off. Camp officials and people in nearby towns often arranged social activities like dances on weekends.

In the 30s, The Army Air Corps and the National Geographic Society conducted experiments at the Stratobowl, a natural flat area surrounded by 500-foot-high cliffs sixteen miles southwest of Rapid City. Because two men first rode a balloon into the earth's stratosphere there in 1935, it is viewed by some as the birthplace of space exploration. Before daylight one morning, Dad's CCC unit arrived by truck to anchor a balloon before launch. "There were hundreds of us all the way around the balloon," Dad said, "and I think a coupla guys on each rope."

A few years ago while browsing through bookshelves in a gift shop in the Black Hills, I found a book with a photo of a balloon launch at the Stratobowl. I don't know if it was taken the day my dad was there, but it looked like a big deal, and I wondered why I had never heard the story before. Or had I, and simply not appreciated it?

Because it would cost money, Dad seldom went home on weekends, but a few times he hitchhiked to Sturgis to see his sister Gladys. Aunt Gladys told me she sometimes sent a little money to Dad, and she liked to make strawberry shortcake for him and his bachelor friends when they dropped in. A few times he found rides all the way home to Perkins County. When his term was up with the CCCs, he reenlisted, because he liked it so well.

By 1936 at the age of 19, he figured he had saved enough money for Aggie, especially if he could supplement it with paid work on campus. He packed his bags.

Dode and Clara borrowed their eldest son R.C.'s Chevy coupe to drive the younger son Orman across the state to Brookings, just twenty miles from the Minnesota state line. There being no Interstate 90 then, they likely drove through Mobridge on Highway 12, where after crossing the Missouri River and passing Rattlesnake Butte, left the arid prairies of west-river behind. Soon, they turned south for about eighty miles to pick up Highway 14 and traveled east for another two hundred miles through the fertile farmland of east river. Ranch work didn't allow for much time off, so after delivering their son to the boys' dorm, Dode and Clara said their goodbyes and good luck and set out for the return trip.

Aggie was part of the college then known as South Dakota State College of Agricultural and Mechanic Arts, which in 1964 became South Dakota State University. Dad beams whenever he talks about Aggie. When I brought up the subject he smiled and said, "Now, that was a school I really enjoyed." Though his time there sounds like college and took place on a college campus, he was enrolled in a high school program, a nine-month curriculum compressed into five so rural kids could work on their parents' ranches. A companion two-year Home Economics program for girls provided classes in cooking and sewing.

Most of Dad's classes took place in the Old North Building, where he studied cattle and hog breeds, cutting up meat, business management, building and equipment maintenance, crops and haying methods; but, he said, "not much about horses, darn it." When he showed me a large manila envelope full of memorabilia from his Aggie days, I was surprised, because his own photos had been destroyed in a house fire in 1947; thankfully, friends and relatives had replaced many. I didn't remember Dad ever talking about being in a play, but I found a playbill listing him in the role of "young son of the family" in the play *Early to Bed, Early to Rise*, a comedy in three acts by William F. Davidson.

I suspect acting interested him far less than sports, where his natural grace and athleticism kicked in. Basketball teams voted him captain all three years at Aggie, and he competed in and won boxing matches, one memorable outdoor one in Rapid City where a huge crowd in surrounding bleachers gathered to watch him defeat a notable out-of-town boxer.

Front and center, Orman Willey, captain of the Aggies basketball team

At first he lived on campus and did janitor work for extra money, but after he got acquainted with Ben and Guy Luttman and their cousin Toots Tollgaard, the four boys moved out of the dorm and rented an apartment together. Dad agreed to be the cook, because he was the only one who knew how, and the rest of the boys said they would buy food. However, that didn't seem to be a problem, because on weekends all of them often traveled about twelve miles south toward Sioux Falls to the Luttman farm. Mrs. Luttman always sent them back to school with their jeans washed and ample supplies of homemade bread, butter, pies, cakes, sides of bacon, and garden vegetables. "She was a real nice lady," my dad said, smiling and shaking his head in wonder.

He gives fatherly status to a teacher at Aggie named Paul Scarborough. "He guided me all the way through," he said. Early on Mr. Scarborough encouraged Dad to upgrade to slacks instead of work jeans for some school events. And Dad said, "He convinced me that the Reserve Officer Training Corps would be good experience." It was required of male college students then and an option for boys in the high school program. Dad signed up and attended classes on first aid, leadership, and military procedures.

Because the school year was shortened to five months, and because of travel expense, Dad seldom went home from Aggie except for the seven-month "summers." He went home only once during his sophomore year, for Thanksgiving when he caught a ride with one of the Dillon boys.

Long summers at home on the ranch meant hard work for Dad, but fun, too, especially when it came to a game called baseball. Small-town rural areas embraced the game and Strool had fielded teams complete with uniforms and umpires since the 1910s. By the 1930s, most towns like Strool, Reva, Buffalo, Bison, and Faith had backstops and a few bleachers. Teams practiced on weekday evenings, but after church on Sundays the whole town gathered at the baseball field for a game with a rival town. Many people sat in their cars parked facing the field to watch. Dad said, "I can still hear my dad hollering at the team. People got pretty stirred up at those games."

"One year," he said, "I organized a team for Strool and we won the division." The win sent them to Watertown for the next level of competition, where they won two games but lost the third, sending them home. Dad said, "And I made the worst error of the game."

He had a tone of deep disappointment bordering on disgust in his voice, so I asked him to tell me what happened.

"I was playing shortstop and I let a ball go right between my legs." He frowned for a moment, but then brightened and said, "But that's the way it goes. You win some, you lose some."

***

In the summer of 1938, while giving his younger brother Aldy rides to Sorum High School, Dad noticed a senior girl named Emma Ruby. When he heard there would be a dance at the school one weekend, he looked forward to it, especially when he heard that Emma and her two sisters would be there.

Mom remembers that night: "The girls, especially Eula Tish, were atwitter about that dance when they found out that Orman had come home from Brookings and would be there." That night Dad probably danced with all three Ruby girls, but remembers for sure that he danced with Emma. For years he has said, "I fell in love with her the first time I danced with her."

At suppertime, he invited her to eat with him. They went to the food table, picked up their paper plates with sandwiches and cake slices and paper cups of coffee and went out to the car. When they were done eating, Dad kissed his date, but she didn't kiss back. "She wasn't exactly friendly about it," Dad said.

Mom shrugged and said, "My mother always told me not to get too close to the boys."

When the band started up again, they went back inside to dance some more. They went to many dances in those years, where bands like the Cressman Brothers and Ike Woodward played "Deep Purple," "Ten Pretty Girls," "Marie," "Margie," "The Missouri Waltz," "The Beer Barrel Polka," and "Dark Town Strutter's Ball." Mom said, "Every dance ended with 'Good Night Sweetheart,' when we always danced with each other. Your dad was the smoothest dancer on the floor," she said, "And all the girls loved dancing with him."

"How did you learn to dance, Dad?" I asked once in a family e-mail.

"I think my sisters must have taught me," he said. "And

I just practiced at the dances."

My sister and I have had the privilege of doing the two-step with him a time or two. My sister wrote, "Dad, I remember that you were a very smooth dancer, because I've danced with you a few times."

Orman Willey received his high school diploma from Aggie in the spring of 1939. His parents sent him the money for a new suit and graduation photo and again made the trip to Brookings to attend the ceremony. Dad said, "Since I was senior class president I had to give a welcoming speech. I was very nervous but managed to get through it." The next day he and his parents met with the athletic coach on campus, who offered Dad work for the following year if he would enroll in college. Dad said, "My folks were in favor, but I had my mind set on going to teacher's college in the Black Hills or ranching, so I turned it down."

Aggie graduation class of 1939; back row, seventh from left, Orman Willey

Aggie Graduation, 1939

Dad returned to west river ranch work determined to save money again, this time for teacher's college. He had so enjoyed sports in high school that he wanted to become a coach. The following fall he enrolled at Black Hills Teachers College in Spearfish (now Black Hills State University), arranging to work out his tuition by tending furnaces and taking care of cows at the college's dairy farm. He had a room in the basement of a dormitory. On some weekends he cleaned and did yard work in Spearfish Canyon at tourist cabins owned by his boss Ma Bridges, Dean of Women.

Around campus, he kept an eye out for Emma Ruby, knowing she had enrolled in the teacher-training program, too. He said, "I couldn't afford to but wanted to take her out to eat or to a movie." My mother said that most of the guys in her high school graduating class were there studying to become teachers.

One evening my dad and a friend saw Emma and her girlfriend Mary Seymour sitting on the hillside near town where the Black Hills Passion Play was being performed. Dad and his friend said hello and sat down next to the girls, and by the time the play ended, the girls had agreed to let the boys walk them home to their small apartment near campus.

After that Dad often walked Mom home from classes, and persuaded her to help him with book reports. Fun times during those days included a ride in the back of a truck with a group of students going to a football game in Deadwood. They took long hikes at Lookout Mountain, and one weekend went with Emma's sister Ruth and her boyfriend, the only one on campus with a car, to Spearfish Canyon for a boat ride and hiking.

By the spring of 1940, Dad teased Mom with, "When are we going to have a blanket party?" Seeing the expression on my face, they both rushed to assure me that meant only "heavy petting." Dad got his wish the night he took Mom to a movie, which impressed her, since no one had much money in those days. They saw *South of the Border* with Gene Autry. Afterwards they took a blanket down by the creek and sat and talked and kissed. By the time they got to Mom's door and kissed goodnight, they agreed they were going steady.

While attending BHTC, Dad learned that he could earn an extra twenty dollars a month with the National Guard Reserves. So he signed up, and in addition to college classes, found himself attending meetings and drills. He hitchhiked to Sturgis for training and once traveled to

Minnesota to a summer training camp.

When my parents graduated in June of 1940 after one year in college, they each had a First Grade Certificate that qualified them to teach grade school. They had to say goodbye and go home, but pledged to write letters over the summer.

When he could borrow a car, Dad drove the thirty miles to the Rubys to visit Mom at Spring Creek Farm. The couple soon faced a problem bigger than physical distance. The closer their relationship became, the colder Mom's father acted. Whenever Dad arrived, her father got into his car and drove down by the creek, where he stayed until his daughter's suitor left. Dad said, "He probably heard that my dad was a drinker and that the Willey boys were pretty wild. R.C. and Noble did get into a few wild escapades, but not me. He was judging me by my brothers and I didn't like that."

Mom said, "My dad wanted me and my sisters to marry young men from his church, but none of them appealed to me like this fun-loving guy. Besides, I didn't love them."

After getting the cold shoulder treatment one too many times, the couple came up with a plan. The next time Dad came calling, Mom would stay upstairs a little longer than necessary, giving Dad a chance to talk to her father.

On the big night, when Dad arrived, Mr. Ruby opened the door for him but turned his back and walked into the living room to sit down at his big desk. Dad followed and sat down in a side chair. After a few moments, he cleared his throat and said, "Sir, it's time you and I had a little talk."

Mr. Ruby looked up and said, "What do you have to say?"

Dad looked him in the eye and said, "Sir, I love your daughter and she loves me and we intend to get married someday. It would mean a lot to both of us to have your approval."

The older man, silent for some moments, moments that seemed like an hour to Dad, finally spoke. To Dad's relief, his future father-in-law reached out and took his hand, shook it firmly, and said, "Thank you for asking me." Mom walked into the room in time to hear her father say to Dad, "I think you're OK." After that, he always greeted Dad with warmth and had nothing but good things to say about him. Before long, Emma Ruby would become Emma Willey. Mom added, in a tone that told me it meant a lot to her, "When we came home from the war, Dad had a big hug for each of us."

Orman Willey took his first teaching job at the Seymour School in Perkins County. "The hardest thing about teaching a one-room school," he said, "was organizing the time for all eight grades." He doesn't remember how many students he had in all, but did have just two in the first grade, one boy and one girl, "a cute little thing." He earned sixty dollars a month, and room and board had to come out of it. His salary was paid in warrants, promissory notes that couldn't always be cashed for face value. It depended on when state funds became available, and many people cashed them in at ten to twenty per cent discount rather than wait.

Mom got a teaching job at the Beck School about twenty miles south of Dad's. He had to spend some weekends fulfilling his commitment to the National Guard Reserve, but when they could find transportation, they saw each other on weekends. When they could afford it, they went to movies, where newsreels reported on the war in Europe: in August of 1940, the English shot down over a hundred German aircraft in separate air attacks over England; the English sank fifty-six German U-boats, and

Germany occupied the Netherlands. It seemed the U.S. would soon get involved.

News on August 31 brought an impending war home to Perkins County; the United States would activate its National Guard. Two young schoolteachers wondered if they would have a future together.

5

Soldier Boy

1941: Germany invades the Soviet Union
Japan attacks Pearl Harbor
U. S. declares war on Japan
In December, rubber rationing goes into effect
Glen Miller's recording of "Chattanooga Choo
Choo" is a million-seller

On February 20, 1941, this article appeared in the
Sturgis Tribune:

Community Bids Farewell to Guardsmen This Week
Company to Entrain Here This Sunday
Company F, 109th Engineers of Sturgis were given to know
that the community is proud of the unit which it is sending
to Camp Claiborne, Louisiana, this weekend, when several
hundred residents turned out for the program Monday night
at the city auditorium at which time a purse of $266.50 was
presented for use in the Company Mess Fund...

A program including a play and musical selections by
the Rapid City recreational project under the direction of
Miss Marie Mylan was followed by a mess style dinner

served by the men of Company F. A dance brought the evening to a close...

Sturgis residents, headed by their high school band, will give their final farewell to Company F at the Northwestern depot here Sunday evening as the men entrain for their year's training at Camp Claiborne, Louisiana. The train will leave the station at 8:15. The band will meet at 7:15...

Sturgis unit is up to full strength with 90 men and three officers. The following mailing address for letters to members of Company F while they are at the camp was given today at headquarters here: Pvt. John Doe, Co. F, 109th Engineers (C), 34th Division, Camp Claiborne, La. APO 34.

When his National Guard unit was activated, Orman Willey resigned his teaching position and reported for active duty in the United States Army. Determined to serve his country, the Dakota cowboy would soon be a soldier.

Orman Willey, far left, boards a train with Company F

Dode and Clara traveled to Sturgis to see their son off. He didn't know how long it would be before he saw them or his sweetheart again, but he understood that his commitment to the Army was for one year. My mother resumed her teaching duties at the Beck School and began to watch the mail for letters from her soldier boy. Dad often closed his letters with, "Keep smilin' and stay in the road."

A few months later, Dad got a chance to see Mom again when her school was out for the summer. He wrote and asked if she would go with Dode and Clara on a 1,500-mile car trip to Louisiana to see him. Aldy, Dad's younger brother and his girlfriend Margo were going along, so my mother packed a suitcase and went, too. When they all got to Louisiana in a 1940 Ford, they stayed with Dad's sister Gladys, who lived in the area with her husband and son Max.

Dad and Mom enjoyed spending time with the family, but they looked for a way to sneak away and have another blanket party, just the two of them. One afternoon they borrowed Dode and Clara's car and drove to Alexandria, where they found a jewelry store and bought a diamond engagement ring. They came across a little park in town and stopped to talk about their future.

After spreading their blanket on the grass, Dad took Mom's hand and said, "Honey, will you be my wife?" After she said yes, he slid the ring onto her finger and kissed her. He said, "I really hope we have kids someday, but remember, I had the mumps when I was a teenager."

"If we never have kids, we could adopt. We'll just have to take that chance," she said. "We'll have each other."

"They say the war will be over soon."

"You'll write real often and let me know where you are? *How* you are?"

"You bet. And we'll get together somehow to get

married."

They took snapshots of each other and went back to the family to tell them they were engaged, producing hugs all around. When his family had to return to South Dakota, saying goodbye came hard, because Dad knew his next assignment would be overseas. But, one by one, he hugged each one, saving his fiancé for last. He gave her an extra hug and one more kiss, and waved as the car pulled away, wondering when, or if, he would see any of them again.

On December 7, the Japanese bombed Pearl Harbor.

The passage of time seems to blend incidents in our memories. In some ways I am amazed that my dad does not remember where he was on the day he heard about the bombing of Pearl Harbor. He remembers it as being the cause of the activation of his National Guard unit, but apparently he was already training for his first tour of duty in Europe. Mom remembers that Sunday clearly; she and her family sat around the radio and listened as F.D.R. gave his "day that will live in infamy" speech.

In January of 1942, Dad and hundreds of other soldiers arrived in Fort Dix, New Jersey, for transport by bus, train and truck to board a troopship bound for Ireland. To a man who grew up in the center of the nation, the ocean and the immense ship impressed Dad. "I couldn't believe I was going to get on that huge thing and go across an entire ocean. We marched to the ship and then walked up a long ramp, each of us carrying a rifle and a large duffle bag with everything we were allowed to take along." On the first deck he saw a big door and beyond it a stairway leading down to a lower deck, where he found his quarters. "Fortunately, I got a lower bunk," he said, after describing the bunks as stacked six high.

Several destroyers accompanied the troop ship when it sailed, but that precaution didn't prevent it from being torpedoed about a hundred miles out, near Nova Scotia. The damage caused the ship to ride lower in the water. "We could hear water lapping at the ship above us," said Dad, "so naturally we wanted to be on a higher deck. A big bunch of us headed up the stairs."

Their commander, William Brown, met them at the top and said, "You men return to your assigned places on this ship." They obeyed but with reluctance and lingering unease. They later realized the commander had done the right thing; he had to maintain order. William Brown later became the principal at my high school, and I remember him as a calm, quiet leader. The damaged ship had to be towed to Halifax. Dad "picked up the next convoy" and made it all the way to Ireland, a trip that took about ten days. Upon landing in Belfast, the troops and their gear were trucked to their assignments; Dad's group to a little town called Enniskillen.

In an army that would not be integrated until 1948, Dad was assigned to command a platoon of black troops that operated a rock quarry. He said, "At first, I wasn't so pleased to be assigned to a unit of black soldiers, but they proved to be good soldiers. They were hard workers, and I had some I'd put up against anybody." For three months they crushed rock for building roads for maneuver training. Peat bog and trees made good bases for roads in Ireland. Soldiers felled trees, cut them in about eight-foot lengths, trimmed them and rip rapped (supported) the road for hundreds of yards, then put dirt and gravel on top. Dad said, "That's the way the Army built roads to move trucks, tanks, and other equipment to the front lines."

"We lived in Army tents," he went on. "Six to a tent camped on a side hill with a gradual slope. Sometimes they had what they called limey floods (downpours) there. One time rainwater washed everything out from under the cots and two men lost booze they had stashed. For weeks those two hunted for their bottles of tequila and I think they found several." He didn't allow drinking on the job, but when the men were off duty, he had nothing to say about it.

In this letter home, my dad tells about his time in Ireland:

Somewhere in Northern Ireland, May 17, 1942

Dearest Folks,

Well, finally I have the opportunity and time to write to you. I did write a card while sailing but don't know whether it was mailed.

Now before I start with the very things I can write about I'm going to say that the censorship is very strict, therefore my topics are limited. But nevertheless I will tell you what I can. By this time you should have received the safe arrival card from Washington so you know that I have been delivered somewhere in Northern Ireland.

We had a real nice trip coming across that big pond and one doesn't realize how big it is until he goes out in the middle. "Water, water everywhere and not a drop to drink." I don't think Columbus was intelligent, I think he was crazy. Many and many hours I spent out on that deck looking for a whale but I never saw one. Some of the boys did though. Our boat was well loaded and certainly much smoother riding than the other one we were on. A few of the boys were quite sick. As long as I stayed in my bunk everything was OK, 2/3 of my time was spent there too. Immediately after we landed we were moved up here to the camp which certainly was a surprise to all I believe. The quarters

are much nicer than the quarters we had in
Claiborne. As for the scenery it is beautiful. One
can plainly see why this country is called the
Emerald isle with all the shrubbery and green grass
the year around. Also some of the most beautiful
trees I've ever seen.

How is everything coming on the old Arrowhead,
Pa? Suppose you are thinking of turning the cattle
out on the range about this time. It just doesn't seem
possible that it is May. All the big farmers are
admiring their large wheat fields too. I wish some of
these people could see a large field once. All the
farming here is done on a real small scale. Seems to
me as though they group together - that is, several
families live and farm the same fields. I can't see
the reason for it either cause the population isn't
very dense. About the people themselves I don't
know too much about them as yet. I do know one
very peculiar thing they do and that is the reverse
order of the position of their eating utensils. One
more strange and very difficult item is the money.
I'm not completely straight on it yet. We had to turn
in all our American money for English and Irish.
When I went to the pay table for my exchange I
didn't know whether I was getting a hundred dollars
or one. Now I'm fairly well familiarized with it ...

... About all we are doing here now is working on
equipment and cleaning up the camp. Suppose when
that is done we will go on a regular training
schedule again.

About the last month's allotment Mother - I hope
you haven't sent it yet. I can't very successfully get
married over here. Ha There isn't any place to
spend the money over here either. Think I will

increase my allotment to $50.00 soon.

Do you know that the vehicles travel on the left side of the road? Yesterday I was hauling trash and it sure seemed odd to pass cars on the right side and meet them and pass them on the left side.

Well folks, I have written everything I can think of for now. Maybe next weekend I can go out and reconnoiter a few more peculiarities.

Hoping this letter finds you all feeling the best. Keep smiling and we'll keep them rolling.

Be sure that R.C. and Letha get to read this letter. Give Nita [first niece] a big kiss for me.

Love, Orman

In late spring of 1942, Dad received orders to return to the States for Officer Candidate School at Ft. Belvoir, Virginia. He had what he called a delay-enroute, which meant he had extra time before he had to report. So he decided to go home and surprise everyone. He arrived in Lemmon, South Dakota, by train. He was wondering how to get to the Arrowhead Ranch where Dode and Clara lived, when he ran into a neighbor of his folks named Nels Fogh. Because an unseasonable snow storm had made the roads hard to travel by car, Nels gave him a ride to his place, and from there the two men rode horseback twelve or fifteen miles to the Willey home.

Dad peeked in the kitchen window and saw his dad sitting at the table, so he tapped on the window. Dode looked up, jumped to his feet, and said, "Oh, there's a soldier boy."

The soldier walked in and Clara and Dode rushed to meet him with bear hugs.

Home on furlough

The next day, the soldier drove thirty miles to see his fiancé. He said, "Her pupils had all gone home, but she was playing the piano. She thought she heard a noise in the cloakroom, and when she got up to investigate, I came around the corner and said, 'Surprise!'"

Mom said, "My mouth flew open and I squealed when I saw my sweetheart. He grabbed me, and that was the beginning of a life full of surprises."

They had only that evening together and no time to plan a wedding, before Dad had to report to base. This time before saying goodbye, they set a date to both look at the moon at the same time, something they would do several times during the war. Dad told me, "Many times, whenever the moon was out, I would look at it and hope your mother would be doing the same. It seemed to help take away missing her so much." He also carried a snapshot of her in his wallet, showing her sitting on a grassy bank of the South Moreau River back home.

On this trip home my dad purchased a 1941 Packard, which he drove back to Ft. Belvoir. He reported in, finished officer training, and was commissioned a second lieutenant.

After completing her second year of teaching, with school closed for the summer, Mom and her sister Ruth took a bus, their first bus ride, from Deadwood to Denver, Colorado, to help their brother Bill and his wife Frances welcome their second baby. Frances taught Mom and Ruth how to ride the streetcar and explore the city when they had free time. On one big building, the sisters often saw recruiting posters for the Women's Auxiliary Army Corps (WAAC). One day while riding the bus, Ruth surprised Mom by pulling the cord for the bus to stop so they could go in the recruiting office and find out more about it. When they walked out , they had both signed up.

Mom wrote to her fiancé to ask what he thought about her enlisting, but by the time she received his reply of, "No, I'd rather you wouldn't. Stay the same sweet girl," it was too late. She had received orders to report for Basic Training at Ft. Des Moines, and was inducted into the WAACs, later changed to WAC (Women's Army Corps).

A few weeks later, Second Lieutenant Orman Willey was enroute to Ft. Leonard Wood, Missouri, to train troops. He had one free night, so he stopped at Ft. Des Moines, hoping to see Mom. He knew she wouldn't be allowed to leave base during Basic Training, but he had to try. He reached her by phone and said, "Hi Honey. Bet you can't guess where I am."

Mom, who had been called to the phone by her first sergeant, said, "I have no idea. Are you in the States?"

"Would you believe I'm right here in town? I'll explain later. Can you get away tonight?"

As it happened, one of Mom's friends was Charge of Quarters (CQ) that night and agreed to call her present at bed check, so Mom agreed to sneak out. Dad was staying at his Aunt Alice and Uncle Roy's house in Des Moines and borrowed their car. He drove through the bases' front gate, to the barracks, and Mom hopped in. To this day they don't know why the guard at the gate didn't stop them, but Mom speculated that it had everything to do with the bars on the shoulders of Dad's uniform.

They drove back to the house, and after my dad's aunt and uncle had gone to bed, they hugged and kissed and talked until four in the morning, for the most part about how and when they could get married and have a normal life together.

But again, after only a few hours together, they had to say goodbye—they weren't getting any better at it. Dad delivered Mom back to the base, hoping the same guard was still at the gate (he was). Fully clothed, Mom crawled into her bunk just in time to hear the bugle play reveille. Four months later she graduated from Cooks and Bakers School, was promoted to staff sergeant, and transferred to Ft. Oglethorpe, Georgia.

Meanwhile, back in Missouri, Dad found he did not like his new job of "chewing butts" of new recruits at Fort Leonard Wood. So, when he saw a notice on a bulletin board asking for volunteers to work on the Alaska-Canadian Highway, he decided to sign up. After a month went by, he saw the notice again but still hadn't heard anything. So, he requested a meeting with his commanding officer to ask what he needed to do to get the assignment. The officer said he'd look into it.

That did it and not long after, Dad reported for duty at Dawson Creek, British Columbia, to work on the Alaskan-Canadian or ALCAN Highway, a 1,522-mile road from

Dawson Creek to Fairbanks, Alaska, built in eight months by 10,000 troops. He was assigned to the 395th General Service Engineer Battalion, which trained troops while improving the highway as far north as the Peace River.

After only two or three months, many of these troops were deemed ready for assignment to the European front. My dad and his unit were sent to Camp Claiborne, Louisiana, for further training for the war in Europe. Dad said, "We had drill contests then, and my platoon won every one." While in Louisiana that time, he arranged with a woman to store his car and a large trunk full of his belongings in her garage. But when he went after the car later, he never did find the trunk that he had stowed in the rafters. When telling me the story, he ended with a sad look and said, "I just had to let the tail go with the hide."

My parents kept trying to get furloughs at the same time so they could get married. They nearly had it arranged for March of 1943, when Dad got bad news about his older brother. After falling from a horse, R.C. had required surgery and had taken a turn for the worse. His kidneys were failing and he was not expected to live long.

Furlough in hand, Dad hurried home, hoping to see his brother again. But his mother met him at the train station, and said, "Your brother is gone." Robert Curtis Willey was 33 years old and left a widow Letha and daughter Venita. He had a ranch of his own after learning the cattle business from Dode. Years later Clara told my mother that losing R.C. had been even harder than losing Dode. In a letter home to her family when R. C. died, my mother wrote, "Dear Mom, May and All, I got your letters today. It certainly is too bad about R.C.; I couldn't hardly believe it, but it's just one of those things that can't be explained or understood." Dad would have liked to spend more time with his grieving family, but soon after the funeral, he had to return to his base.

In their letters my parents continued to search for a way to get married. Finally, in June of 1943, with furloughs arranged at the same time, they traveled home to be wed. It would be great, they thought, to meet in Chicago and travel the rest of the way home together.

When Dad rolled into the train depot in Chicago, he expected to hop off and find his fiancé waiting. But he couldn't find Mom anywhere. He walked back and forth along the platform looking for the right woman in uniform. After a while he sat down on a bench thinking she might walk by any minute. That didn't work, so he jumped up and walked to each end of the platform again. After he heard someone being paged over a loudspeaker, he tried that, but no one responded. Still no Emma anywhere. Had he misunderstood which day she planned to travel? Or which train? He heard his train being announced. He'd have to go on home without her. He boarded and hoped she would already be home when he got there.

6

Groom

*1943: "People Will Say We're In Love" is a hit
    song*
*Shoes, canned goods, meat, cheese and fat are
    rationed*
Allied forces invade Sicily and bomb Rome
Italy surrenders to the Allies
For Whom the Bell Tolls *plays at the movies*

To this day, my parents give each other a bad time about not finding each other at the Chicago train station. Dad teases, "Maybe you didn't try hard enough to find me." Mom says, "Maybe you didn't try hard enough to find *me*!" But Dad always saves the best line for last: "I thought I was safe, but you waded the creek to get me!"

On that day in Chicago he hoped their missing each other hadn't been a bad omen. This was the second time they strategized for a trip home to tie the knot, and this time it had to happen. Home at last, he called the Rubys to see if his fiancé had arrived. She hadn't, but they expected her the next day, and her brother Richard would pick her up at the train depot in Rapid City. So, he must have misunderstood which day she'd be in Chicago, or she got there late, or— there was nothing for the prospective bridegroom to do but relax and visit with his family. He hadn't seen his fiancé for nine months; he guessed he could wait one more day.

The next day in late afternoon, when his mother's phone rang, he watched as she walked to the phone on the wall and listened as she answered it. She spoke briefly into the phone and then beckoned to her son Orman, smiling. "Someone says she heard you got home yesterday." Into the phone she said, "Here he is, Em."

My dad grabbed the phone and said, "So there you are. Where were you in Chicago?"

"Where were *you*? I'm so glad you're home," she said. "At the train station I thought every man in uniform must be you. I barely made it to my next train on time. I even tried to page you."

"I tried to page you, too, but finally decided you'd gone home without me. I guess I got there ahead of you. Well, we're here now. Let's get this show on the road."

"When will I get to see you?"

"How about tomorrow? I'll come down right after breakfast, and we'll have all day to make plans."

Years later he admitted to having doubts at the time about getting married during wartime. What if he went overseas again? What if he never came back? Should he talk to Emma about these thoughts?

The next morning when he drove his Packard into the Ruby yard, Emma ran out to meet him. She jumped into his arms almost before he got out of the car, and they spent several minutes together, just the two of them.

Finally, they had to go into the house and after hugs and handshakes all around, everyone sat down in the living room to catch up. But soon my mother's parents and sister May left the room so the couple could be alone to plan their wedding.

My mother said, "We can ask May to be the bridesmaid. And her boyfriend Cliff Hathaway the best man. What do you think?"

"Fine," he said. "Let's ask May to come in and then call Cliff."

That done, my mother said, "What about wedding rings?"

"How about that jewelry store in Lemmon?" said the prospective groom, hardly believing this was happening. No one had expressed a single doubt about them getting married. They jumped into the car and drove northeast about eighty miles to Lemmon to buy wedding bands. Mom also found a navy-blue dress with a white lace collar for her bridesmaid. She and Dad would be married in their dress uniforms, because wartime regulations required them to wear uniforms in public. They drove forty miles southwest to Bison, the county seat, for a license. They met with the Lutheran minister, Reverend Solberg, who agreed to marry them on June 12 at the American Lutheran Church.

Luckily they had enough gas ration coupons for this gallivanting, because they were both in the military. Late in the day, after many miles and numerous decisions made, my dad returned my mother home to Spring Creek Farm, kissed her goodbye, and said, "I'll see you in a couple of days, Honey."

"Won't be long now," she said. That gave each of them a little time to spend with their families before leaving again for their war assignments.

It rained hard all day on June 11. On the morning of June 12 rain continued to fall. The dirt roads of Perkins County turned into a slippery mess as they always do when wet. Folks around those parts call it gumbo.

At the Ruby house, the bride and her sister glanced out the windows, wondering if the best man would make it through. He was supposed to pick them up first.

"He'll have to plow mud all the way," said my mother.

May said, "Well, we'd better get ready in case he does make it." They bustled around, often passing a window to watch for Cliff's 1938 Chevy coupe.

Soon, he drove into the yard, heartily welcomed by two young women prepared for a wedding, questions flying before he could get past the entryway.

My mother said, "Will we be able to get to the Willeys or to Bison, Cliff?"

"Do you think we should go on?" said May.

Hat in hand, Cliff grinned, showing his deep dimples. "It's my job to get you to the altar, Em. We can take to the prairie if we need to. You girls willing to give it a try?"

"Of course," they said and ran upstairs to get their coats and the bride's suitcase.

The three of them piled into the Chevy and struck out for the Willeys to collect the groom. Cliff veered off-road onto the prairie more than once to avoid the worst gumbo, but the car got stuck several times. Each time the girls had to get out and push. On top of that, the car overheated once, so they had to get rain water out of a ditch for the radiator.

Meanwhile, back at the ranch—doubts about it being a good day for a wedding had also surfaced at the Willey house. Dode had gone out to the barn earlier to harness his team of horses for hauling hay, but had come back into the house hoping for the rain to taper off some. To pass the time he sat down for a game of Cribbage with his son.

Dad gathered the dealt cards, looked at his hand, and said, "I hope this weather isn't going to stop me from marrying that girl." He looked out the window again. "The kids should be here by now, shouldn't they?"

After a puff from his pipe, Dode said, "They'll either drive in or they won't."

When the dogs started barking, everyone headed for the windows. They couldn't see a thing, but the dogs continued their ruckus, so they all went out to the yard. Here came the bride, bridesmaid and best man trooping toward the house. When they got within earshot, Cliff said, "We left the car in the 'crick'."

"The water was really high," May said, "but Cliff said, 'We can't stop now,' and started across." She beamed at him.

"The car stalled in the middle," Em said, "and water ran over the floorboards. We had to take off our shoes and wade the rest of the way."

Dode grabbed his coat and turned toward the barn. "Come on boys. I've got the team already harnessed. Let's pull that car to higher ground."

Clara said, "Come in out of this rain, girls." While the men rescued the Chevy, inside the house Clara checked her roast and peeled potatoes, while the girls spot-cleaned their mud-splashed wedding clothes and washed out their stockings. They hung them up by the stove, hoping they would have time to dry.

After the men came in, Clara served lunch, probably wishing she could hang onto her company a little longer. She and Dode had lost their eldest son R.C. just three months earlier. Now Orman was getting married and going away again for who knew how long. I wondered why Dode and Clara or my mother's parents didn't go to the wedding that day. When I asked, Mom said, "There wasn't time." I suppose they talked about it, but the logistics of getting everyone to Bison and back home again would be difficult because of the short notice, bad weather and gas rationing.

Cliff Hathaway, Orman Willey, Emma Ruby, and May Ruby
made it to the church on time.

Anxious to get going right after lunch, the wedding
party completed a quick round of goodbyes. My parents got
into the Packard and Cliff and May followed in the Chevy.
They traveled to the church in Bison with no problems, and
the ceremony didn't take long. Afterwards May and Cliff
left for home right away, because rain continued to fall and
the roads could only get worse. The newlyweds drove out
of Bison, married at last.

Now they would have a honeymoon, five days of travel
to their respective camps, my mother to Ft. Oglethorpe in
Georgia and my dad to Camp Claiborne, Louisiana. They
got stuck once more in gumbo that day, but finally made it
to Belle Fourche, South Dakota, where they stayed in a
hotel called the Hampton. The next morning they
breakfasted in a little restaurant around the corner. On their
way east they stopped in Piedmont not far from Rapid City,
to see Orman's brother Noble (Dad called him Nibs) and
his wife Margie, who by then had increased their family to
four with Dolyce Ann and Jerry Dean. In Rapid City they

stopped for a few minutes to see his other brother Aldy and his wife Margo, married just over a year.

They continued east on paved highways, expecting few problems for the several days remaining for their honeymoon.

Until they had a flat tire.

Dad changed the tire but knew the spare would never make it all the way to Georgia. They still had gas coupons, but no tire coupons. How would they get a new tire? His charm and a garage owner in Mitchell saved the day. When he understood that these people, both in uniform, were newlyweds on their way to report for duty, he said he would make an exception.

New tire installed, he added, "And thanks for fighting this darn war for all of us."

The newlyweds stopped in Des Moines, Iowa, to visit Dad's Aunt Alice and Uncle Roy, and the following morning had a wedding picture taken. They also sent this letter home:

Des Moines, Iowa, June 15, 1943

Dear Folks,

Just a few lines this morning to tell you that we arrived here in Des Moines safely. We have had good luck so far with the exception of one blowout. We had to spend all forenoon in Mitchell yesterday trying to get a tire and finally ended up with a brand new one, so now we have smooth sailing again. We had to put on chains between Strool and Buffalo but didn't have any trouble.

We passed Richard and Arlene on the way to Rapid. We stopped there a couple hours to see Aldy and Margaret [Margo].

Needless to say, we have had a wonderful time.
How did you and Cliff get back home May: we
were sort of worried. We didn't even thank you kids
for standing up with us. We both thought of it
afterwards, and we really do appreciate what you
kids went through to get us married. Maybe we can
do the same for you some day. Sure hope Cliff's car
is OK after all the trouble.

We expect to leave here about noon again. I will
write you again when we get down there.

Love, Em and Orm

P.S. We saw Ruth, went out to Ormie's Aunt
Alice's for dinner and are on our way again she was
tickled to see us and looking real good.

Ormie wants to write a few lines but is driving
and won't trust me to drive while he writes so will
dictate to me.

Quote: "Em has written all the news so about all
I have to say is, we're having a grand and glorious
time, and wish it could go on forever. We expect to
be in Tennessee sometime tomorrow afternoon.
Hope everything goes along as smoothly as it has so
far, especially the nights. Ha ha

We had a grand visit in Des Moines with Ruth
and Aunt Alice, and managed to have our pictures
taken. Hope they turn out all right.

I've run out of news and my stenographer is
getting tired so will sign off for this time. We will
be back on the same station, some time tomorrow
evening, so goodbye for now." Unquote.

Love from Orm and Em

The rest of the trip went smoothly, but sometimes the bride had to get used to her new husband's teasing. He often whistled at females on the streets of little towns they drove through. On the six hundred miles from Des Moines to Fort Oglethorpe, they saw a few sights and stayed in motels. Emma wrote later, "By the time we got to Fort Oglethorpe we knew each other well."

I thought they might have talked as they rode along about having to say goodbye in a few days, but they avoided the subject and, though their bases were nearly six hundred miles apart, talked about getting together on weekend passes later.

When they arrived in Georgia, ready or not, they had to say goodbye, having no idea when they would see each other again. Having no choice, my dad kissed his new wife goodbye and continued on to Louisiana alone.

After a lonely drive, he reported in and found important news waiting for him. He searched for a phone to call his wife. "Hi, Sweetheart. I made it here, but it sure was lonely without you. I'm afraid I have bad news. I have orders to sail for Europe right away."

"Overseas again?" she said. "All those plans to meet on weekends will never happen."

"Not for a while anyway. We'll just have to wait until this darn war is over. Then we'll make up for lost time."

"I hope you write me lots of letters and I hope they make it to me."

"I will. And remember, when you look at the moon, I'll be looking at it, too."

In June of 1943, my dad packed his bags again. Everything he wanted to take along had to fit into a regulation duffle bag. In his wallet, he still carried the snapshot of his wife. At Fort Dix, New Jersey, the men climbed onto trucks that ferried them to a troop ship. Other troops arrived by train, and after everyone and his gear was loaded, the ship set sail for England.

Because this was a much bigger ship than the one my dad rode the first time overseas, the ocean crossing took only five days instead of ten, and the ride was smoother. In berthing areas, the ship's walls were lined with three levels of bunks with ladders leading up to them. A bunk was merely a piece of canvas attached to the wall with a metal-pipe frame. "It was about three feet wide and plenty long, about six feet," said my dad. "I got quite comfortable with it. Each guy had his own locker near his bunk and a space to store his duffle. We had to shower in salt water, which took some getting used to, because it was impossible to work up any suds. That was a beautiful trip with nice weather most of the way. We even sat on the deck, and I got the best tan I ever had."

They ate meals in the mess hall, where they stood at belly-high tables that had ridges at the edges to keep things from sliding off if the ship listed. Dad said, "That only happened a couple of times, though, and we had all kinds of good food."

Soon after Dad went overseas, Mom got orders for Europe, too. She wrote a letter to him suggesting that once she got there, perhaps they would be able to get together in some way. But a Dakota blizzard kept her from returning to base after a furlough home, and another WAC took her place on the overseas assignment. She never got to Europe.

Orm and Em would not see each other again for more than two years.

7

Soldiering On

1944: In June, Allied Forces invade Normandy,
*   France, on D-Day*
Paris is liberated in August
Franklin D. Roosevelt is elected for a fourth
*   term*
"Mairzy Doats" is a popular song
The White Cliffs of Dover *is playing at the*
*   movies*

On his way overseas the second time, Lt. Orman Willey spent part of his time on board ship in briefings to prepare for impending duties. Dad said, "They didn't tell us everything right away, especially if they knew it might be hard to deal with." Upon arrival in England, he was assigned to Company E of the 95th Engineers, 34th Division. He would eventually take part in the Normandy, Southern France, Rhineland, Ardennes and Central Europe campaigns.

Wherever he went, he watched the mail for letters from

his new wife. He wrote to her almost every week, but they both discovered that the mail didn't always go through. "When you were on a mission," Dad said, "you might not get your mail for a month or even two." And then they would get several letters at once. Neither of my parents remembers telephones being readily available then, and besides, long distance rates were high. Both report that they and their comrades treasured mail call. A first sergeant usually announced it at the mess hall. He would bark a name, and each soldier would go forward and grab his packet of letters. Dad said, "I always tried to go back to my quarters to read my mail in private." He got letters from his mother and sisters, and best of all, his wife.

My cousin Dolyce Wood, Dad's niece by his older brother Noble, found a V-Mail from my dad to her parents in a box of mementos they had kept. I am so thankful she shared it with me, because I believe it is the only surviving letter my dad wrote during his second tour overseas. What a gift to see my Dad's actual words in his own beautiful penmanship. Here it is in actual size, and because it is hard to read, text follows (Dad calls his brother Noble, Nibs):

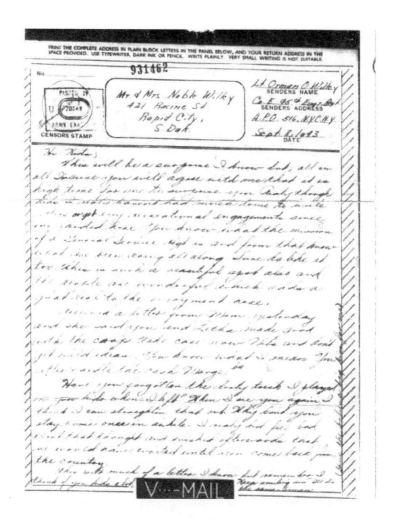

Hi Kids;

    This will be a surprise I know but all in all I'm sure you will agree with me that it is high time for me to surprise you. Really though kids I really haven't had much time to write letters or get any recreational engagements since we landed here. You know what the mission of a General Service Rpt is and from that know what I've been doing all along. Sure do like it too. This is such a beautiful spot also and the people are wonderful which adds a great deal into the enjoyment here.

Received a letter from Mom and she said you and Letha made good with the crops. Take care now Nibs and don't get wild ideas. You know what I mean. You better handle the cash Marge. Ha

Have you forgotten the dirty trick I played on you kids when I left? When I see you again I think I can straighten that out. Why don't you stay home once in awhile? I really did feel bad about that thought [sic] and wished afterwards that we would have waited until you came back from the country.

This isn't much of a letter I know but remember I think of you kids a lot. Keep smiling and I'll do the same. -Orman

When I showed this piece of his history to my dad, he read it and said, "I wrote to Nibs and Aldy quite a bit, you see, because I was lonesome for them."

V-mail saved shipping space for war materials, because 37 mailbags carrying 150,000 one-page letters and weighing 2,575 pounds could be replaced by one bag weighing 45 pounds. Military personnel wrote letters on normal-size forms, the letters were reduced to small images, and later printed larger for the recipient.

During their separation my parents saved many of each other's letters, but they all burned, along with their uniforms, in the house fire of 1947. That loss included a rifle that my dad once sent home from Europe picked up in an area in which Germans had camped and vacated.

After weeks of classes and briefings on their mission, Dad's unit began practicing specialized field exercises.

When they were ready, on the second day of the D-Day invasion, they crossed the English Channel in big ships. After climbing into pontoon boats to get closer to the beach, they then had to walk in water the rest of the way. Dad held the edge of his flat hand at chest level to show me how deep the water was. He said, "The Germans had already been pushed back, so when we got there, all we saw was beach. A little further in we came to some brushy areas. We had to wait for vehicles and equipment, so we set up a bivouac camp. When the vehicles arrived, we moved inland through France."

They built and repaired roads, railroads and bridges to keep supplies going to the front lines. At one time they were sent to an old sawmill in the woods where they spent several days cutting and trimming logs for a bridge.

Orman Willey on right, somewhere in Europe

The Germans frequently targeted their operations and tried to knock them out. Once the unit was building a bridge and a Quonset hut on its edge. My dad said, "We could hear buzz bombs coming for miles but couldn't take cover, because we didn't know where they would land. That time I thought we were done for." But they got lucky, because the bomb hit the water and the explosion only splashed water on them. He said the buzz bombs sounded like small single-engine airplanes. They were the German version of self-propelled missiles, unmanned rockets launched from a pad and directed by a gyroscope toward a target. They carried about five hundred pounds of explosive and when they ran out of fuel, they landed and blew up.

At some point my dad's unit arrived at the Liege River. They were working toward Berlin but never got there. He said, "Typically, the Infantry went ahead of our unit and took the worst of the fire. Some towns they went through were so flattened by bombing that we had to use bulldozers to get through."

Dad has forever been thankful he never had to shoot or kill anyone while serving in the Army. He did spend hours on the rifle range in training and said, "I don't know if you want this kind of information, but I earned every medal available there."

His men worked for a time on a large building and camped out in a complex nearby that was like an old college campus with a large open area in the middle. "That's where we had our tents set up," he said. A bomb landed within that area one night, shearing off the top of the tent in a platoon next to them. A four-foot high wall of sandbags around the tent saved the guys inside, because they were sleeping behind the wall.

In Belgium, Dad was assigned to supervise the guarding of several hundred German prisoners of war for three nights. It was a temporary facility with prisoners kept in netting corrals. Frequently, someone shouted that prisoners were escaping, and he and his men heard small arms fire. He said, "Several times we were under fire from our own troops, when they shot at the enemy trying to get out." The look on his face said, "I did not like that situation one bit."

One time when they heard noises from the nearby woods, he sent a corporal around one side of the complex and he took the other. They agreed they would fire three shots into the air at a specific time, hoping that would scare off whoever was advancing on them. After firing, they didn't hear any more noises, so they returned to their posts. The next morning, they found several cows grazing nearby and decided that was all they'd heard in the woods the day before.

Regulations prohibited American soldiers from making any contact with the German prisoners, requiring them to stay twenty feet away. But prisoners often motioned to them. "They would try to get information out of us." Dad is thankful he never had to interrogate the prisoners. He doesn't remember where he and his men went after being pulled away from the prison-guard duty, but said, "I was sure tickled to get out of there." I asked if the guys he was with felt the same way, and he said, "You bet."

***

Once, when he was directing a convoy of Army vehicles led by a motorcycle, Dad received the only physical injury of his service, a whiplash. As he stood facing forward in the first vehicle of his convoy, a hand went up in the convoy ahead to hold up. He tried to stop his convoy, but the guy driving the vehicle behind him didn't get the message and rammed into his, causing him to fall back into the seat. Since then any painful back twinge makes him appreciate that his injuries were nothing compared to the great losses and supreme sacrifices suffered by other families during that war or others since.

***

Two and a half years is a long time for a married couple to be separated, and though rarely talked about, both of my parents experienced temptations. While in France, my dad met a young woman who reminded him of my mother. He had been invited to a French family's home for meals, which he enjoyed very much. The young woman was someone's niece, and he got the impression they hoped he would take to her. But apparently he kept things on the up-and-up by writing to Mom and teasing her about his French "girlfriend."

During her WAC years, my mother had a male friend, who wanted her to take their relationship to a more romantic level, but she never let it happen. She danced with him and talked to him about work, because he had the same job she did cooking for the troops. She said, "I've often wondered what happened to him after the war. He was such a nice man and good friend."

***

In the spring of 1945, by now a First Lieutenant, my dad got orders to go back to the States for rehabilitation and reassignment. On the ship (possibly the Queen Mary or Queen Elizabeth) with an entire battalion of seven hundred men, he shared a stateroom with another officer. They also enjoyed their own dining room with sit-down tables. From the rumor grapevine, they heard that their next assignment would be "somewhere in the Pacific."

But while at sea Dad heard an announcement that was, "one of the happiest moments of my life." A voice blared from the ship's loudspeaker announcing that Hitler's army had surrendered and the war in Europe was over. "There was such a whoopin' and hollerin' you wouldn't believe."

Even before they reached the United States, they got official word that qualified soldiers who wanted to could be discharged soon after landing. When asked if he had mixed feelings about what to do, my dad said, "No question I wanted out." Even though he was up for captain, he was ready to return to civilian life. "After all, I'd been told when I signed up it would be for a year." It had been four years, over two since he'd seen his wife. Knowing my dad, I can imagine him looking for a quiet nook or cranny on that ship and gazing at the photo of his wife. Years later he would admit that the "pass the buck" mentality of the Army made him question where he stood.

When the ship neared the harbor in New York, the announcer on the loud speaker had another message—the Statue of Liberty had been sighted. Servicemen lined the decks to gaze at the symbol of liberty they had all helped to protect. Dad said, "She was a fantastic sight."

After disembarkment, he saw lines of soldiers waiting for phones. When he got his turn, his first call was to his wife, stationed then at Dow Field, Maine. She got called to the phone from the officer's club, where she was having a pitcher of beer with friends to celebrate war's end. She told Dad she thought she could get an emergency furlough so they could meet in Sparta, Wisconsin, where he would be mustered out of the Army at Fort McCoy. She returned to her friends and ordered another pitcher of beer, because now she had even bigger news to celebrate.

Arrangements made, my dad boarded a troop train for Sparta. When he got there, he hopped off the train and began searching the crowd for a certain woman in uniform. The town was swimming with GIs, because this was not the first trainload to arrive. He didn't see my mother anywhere. He stepped into a small hotel and asked if she may have already checked in. They had no guests named Emma Willey—no vacancies either.

He continued walking up and down the streets for what seemed like miles, wondering what to do next. Would they miss each other like they had at the Chicago train station that time? Why in the world hadn't they made a better plan for finding each other?

Finally at another hotel, a woman told him that a lady in uniform had asked for him by name. He might be getting somewhere. Then, across the street, he saw his wife carrying a suitcase. He jogged across the street, walked up behind her, and tapped her on the shoulder. "Where do you think you're going?"

She turned around, dropped her suitcase, and said, "I'm looking for a place to spend the night with you," and wrapped her arms around his neck. She leaned back, searching his face. "I wondered if I'd recognize you after all this time. You look better than ever and just the same."

"I was afraid I'd missed you again in a train station," he said. He kissed her.

"Me too," she said. "It took me all night and all day yesterday to get here."

He encircled her waist with his arms, grinned and said, "What'll we do now?"

"A clerk at the hotel told me about a private home where I might be able to rent a room. That's where I was going."

He had already picked up her suitcase. They rented an

attic room with a bathroom down the hall, and settled in to get reacquainted. My dad said, "We weren't shy at all and just loved each other." The war was over and they were going home. Soon, Emma would be out of the WACs and God willing, they could start a family.

They talked for hours about what they had been doing in their separate parts of the world and about civilian life opening to them. When he lit a cigarette, my dad was surprised to find that his wife wanted one, too. She'd been trying to convince herself cigarettes would be a thing of the past once she was out of the service, and never did smoke in front of her parents.

Eventually they got hungry, so he pulled on his clothes and went out to find food. He came back with two hamburgers and two beers, their first meal together since saying goodbye at Fort Oglethorpe at the end of their honeymoon.

A day or so later, with his discharge papers in hand, my parents boarded a train for Minneapolis, and from there took a commercial plane to Rapid City, South Dakota. Dad's brother Aldy picked them up and took them to his house, where Dad picked up his 1941 Packard. For about a week the ex-soldier and his military wife visited their families around the Black Hills and Perkins County.

When it was time for Mom to report back to Dow Field in Maine, they decided that Dad would go along, which meant another train ride. Figuring they hadn't yet had much private time as a couple, they stopped over for a couple of honeymoon nights in a big hotel in downtown Chicago, including breakfast in bed.

In Maine, they rented a small apartment in Bangor, where they once invited a bunch of Mom's WAC friends for a party. She wanted to get out of the service, too, and requested a discharge. When she signed up, it had been "for the duration." She later wrote of her adventures in the WACS in *Beyond the Silent Prairie* (PublishAmerica, 2006): "I wouldn't trade my service experience for anything, but I didn't see much future there for women."

After about a week she became a civilian, too. To get back home to South Dakota, Dad used "officer's privilege" and hitchhiked a ride for them on a C-47 transport plane out of Dow Field that got them to Granier Field, New Hampshire. From there they caught a B-17 bomber headed for Detroit, Michigan. When they boarded, there were no seats, so they sat on their suitcases by the window. Soon after take-off, they saw what looked like misty rain going by the window and wondered why the pilot began to maneuver the plane to tip the wings.

The co-pilot appeared and said, "You'd better put on parachutes. We may have to make an emergency landing."

Dad got into his parachute immediately and helped Mom into hers. As he checked and rechecked straps, she shouted, "If we have to jump, you'll have to pull the cord for me, because I'll probably pass out."

Dad said, "Okay, I will." He looked into her eyes. "We're not going down with this plane, I'll tell you that right now."

They never had to jump, for the pilot found a place to land the plane, and reported that a cap on one of the gas tanks had not been securely fastened. After that was corrected, my parents climbed back on and flew on to Detroit, where, having had enough flying adventures, they boarded another train for home.

Finally, though the war would continue in the Pacific for months yet, World War II was over for this young couple from the plains. They had done their duty. They were together again. They were home.

But, as the old World War I song goes, how ya gonna

keep 'em down on the farm?

8

Home Boy

1945: Harry Truman assumes presidency after
F.D. Roosevelt dies
May 8 is Victory in Europe Day
Atomic bombs are dropped in Japan
Rationing ends
"It's Been a Long Long Time" is a popular
song

In the summer of 1945, when their train pulled into the depot in Rapid City, Orman Willey hopped to the ground and turned around to take his wife's hand as she stepped down. "Welcome home," he said with a smile. This time they hoped to be home from the war for good. On the radio, they often heard a song called "Gotta Make Up for Long Lost Time" and set about doing just that. To this day they can sing every verse. My dad's brother Aldy picked them up and drove them to the Arrowhead Ranch, where Dode and Clara still lived and where the Packard had been stored in the barn. Dad figured he'd work for his dad until he could buy his own ranch. He still had the nine head of cattle purchased from his sister-in-law Letha after R.C. died.

My dad looked forward to wearing civilian clothes again, but as long as he wore his uniform, people came up to him and welcomed him home, often asking what he did in the war. With pride he told them he built bridges in Germany so the troops could get through. My mother said she and her WAC friends had always been proud to walk down any street in uniform during the war; however, sometimes people did say that women in uniform, "should be home where they belong." But after the war, Mom said, "I couldn't get out of uniform fast enough." I get the feeling that both of my parents considered their military service an amazing adventure and opportunity to help their country, but they always expected to return to their own lives afterwards.

As always, ranch life included going to dances. At a dance in Strool one night, Dad ran into a group of kids that he had taught in the one-room grade school before enlisting. Now in high school, they spotted him and full of smiles, ran up saying, "Mr. Willey, do you remember us?"

Dad laughed and kidded them, saying, "I sure do. You're the ones who hid books in the rafters of the outhouse so you could go out and look up answers during tests."

Rapid City bustled after the war, and Dad began to wonder if he could make more money there. The town nearly doubled in population between 1940 and 1948, reaching 27,000, partly because of the Army air base (it later became Ellsworth Air Force Base). Housing was scarce, but my parents decided to move and rented a small apartment in the back of the same house as Aldy and Margo. Until he could find something better, my dad took a job at a filling station. He could always return to the ranch if nothing better panned out.

Before enlisting in the WACs, my mother had helped her mother and sisters cook for a big family. As a mess sergeant she had managed a kitchen staff that cooked for hundreds. Now, in her little apartment, she was learning to cook for two. Moreover, she yearned to cook for three— she wanted a baby. Knowing it might not be possible because of that case of mumps Dad had as a teen, she kept hoping anyway.

Finally, a missed period made her wonder if she might possibly get to be a mother after all. She wanted to be sure before telling my dad and getting his hopes up and went to the doctor, who confirmed the pregnancy. She wondered why the exam had to be so painful, but decided not to worry and hurried home to tell her husband he was going to be a daddy.

Afraid to believe the news, he said, "No kidding? The mumps didn't make me sterile?"

"No, I'm not kidding. The doctor said I'm going to have a baby."

"Oh Honey, that's so wonderful," he said, hugging her. Later he grinned and looked at her sideways. "Are you sure the bread man didn't pay you a visit?"

"Stop that, you rascal!" she said, slapping at his arm.

He took her into his arms. "You know I was just teasing."

That night they stayed up late with new blessings to count. They talked about how much fun it would be to tell their families the news. Thanksgiving, when the family would be together around the table, would be the perfect time.

The next morning Dad kissed Mom goodbye and left for work. When he got home for lunch, he knew something was wrong, because his wife was still in bed and looked paler than the white sheets. He sat down beside her on the bed and said, "What's wrong, Honey?"

"I've been bleeding all morning," she said, "but I've tried to stay in bed and stay real still. I just know that doctor caused this by the way he examined me." She paused to get her voice past the lump in her throat. "I was even afraid to walk over to the neighbors to use their phone." She and Dad didn't have one yet, and Aldy and Margo had been gone all day.

My dad ran to another neighbor and called the doctor, who said, "Get your wife to the hospital immediately." Dad found a stack of towels and put them in the car for Mom to sit on as they drove to the hospital. Later, the doctor confirmed that she had miscarried.

Three days later on the day before Thanksgiving in 1945, his wife released from the hospital, my dad took her home to their quiet little apartment. Unable to face a festive family dinner, Dad said, "You don't have to cook either, Honey." They had to process the news themselves before sharing with others and went to the Virginia Café, just the two of them.

***

One day when my dad got home from work, he said, "How'd you like to go on a nice trip to Oregon?"

"I'd like to a lot," said Mom, "because we haven't had enough honeymoon yet." She started thinking about what to pack, but thought of something else. "What about your job?"

"They said I could take a leave of absence and go back to work when we get back."

"Then, let's go."

"Can you be ready by tomorrow? Get a wiggle on."

But the next day she was surprised to find out that they wouldn't be traveling alone. Always thinking of others, her husband had invited his sister Gladys and her two kids Max and Bonnie Karen (B. K. for short) to go with them to San Francisco, where her husband Jack had found work after the war. Eventually, things worked out fine. They all had a fun trip to Hillsboro, Oregon, to see Dad and Gladys's sister Bonnie and her husband Russ, whom they hadn't seen since the war ended. From there they traveled to San Francisco, where Gladys and kids hooked up with Jack, and Mom and Dad had another honeymoon after all, taking a longer way home just the two of them.

By Christmas, my parents had moved into a furnished one-bedroom house with more room, so they invited the Willey family for Christmas. Dad's brothers and their wives had produced several grandchildren for Dode and Clara by then, so thirteen people showed up for the holiday dinner: Dode and Clara with Dode's sister Alice visiting from Iowa; Aldy and Margo and son Dennis from next-door; and from Piedmont, Noble and Marge with Dolyce, Jerry (Buckshot) and Ray (BB shot, later shortened to Beeb).

***

In the spring of 1946, a man came into the filling station where Dad worked and said he was looking for men to help build a dam near Fort Peck, Montana. It would be one of the world's largest hydroelectric earth-filled dams and improve flood control and irrigation. When the man said the pay would be two dollars an hour, more than he was making, Dad got interested.

His wife didn't object and said later, "I had to go with

the breadwinner." So they gave up their furnished house, piled everything they owned into the Packard, and drove to Montana for the summer. They bought a used bed, table, and chairs and lived in one of four apartments in a remodeled barracks. They became lifelong friends with two couples they met there: John and Esther Fuller and Ray and Esther Shepherd, and often played Whist when the husbands were off work.

Dad drove a huge earth-moving machine called a Terra Cobra and has always said, "I moved a lot of dirt on that job." He once got fired for three days for running over a stake after being warned not to, when the foreman said, "Willey, go take a little vacation." So it seemed a good time to check out the Calgary Stampede in Calgary, Alberta, Canada.

In the early spring of 1946, Mom once again got pregnant. Again, hope arose that she and Dad would have a family. She took things very easy, and the pregnancy proceeded with no problems. Her friend Esther Fuller was pregnant, too, so they drove to Glasgow to doctor appointments together.

In Montana Dad developed a passion for catching walleye pike in the Missouri River. He wanted to go fishing every weekend, so his wife decided she'd better develop the habit or be a fishing widow. It became a lifelong hobby for them both, pursued in many states across America during active retirement years.

As expected, work on the Fort Peck dam ended in the fall. After six months, my dad was earning three dollars an hour and my parents had a small savings. It was time to go home, so they threw away their crepe paper "curtains" (strips of crepe paper gathered and tacked around a window frame), sold their used furniture back to the same store, and drove home to South Dakota.

By this time Dode and Clara were ready to take life a little easier, so Dad decided to go into the farming and cattle business with his dad. He traded the Packard for a new 1946 one-ton Ford pickup truck, tickled that the Packard was still worth a thousand dollars, the same he had paid for it during the war. They bought a 23-foot trailer house and set it up near the ranch house. Neither house had a bathroom as outhouses were still in use in those parts. Dad settled in to the ranch routine and Mom enjoyed her new little house and waiting for their baby to arrive. She got so big that Dode grinned and used his favorite line when spying a pregnant woman: "You must've swallowed a watermelon seed, Em."

About this time, my dad talked to Andy Thybo, the owner of the 1,300-acre Arrowhead Ranch where they lived and worked, about buying it. Andy seemed willing, so Dad took a trip to town to have a visit with the banker, but was turned down for a loan, because he did not have enough equity. He decided to continue working for Thybo and save money until he had enough to buy a ranch.

On December 2, 1946, Mom had a few intermittent pains. Not sure they were labor pains, my parents decided to travel at least part of the way to Rapid City and the hospital. They would stop by Mom's sister May's place. May, the bridesmaid at my parent's wedding, had by this time married Cliff, Dad's best man. They had brought home a new baby girl Bonita May only four months earlier.

When Mom and Dad got to May and Cliff's, May said, "I think you should keep going to the hospital. It can happen fast."

Cliff agreed. "Ya, it's still an hour and a half from here."

"Don't worry," said Mom. "We'll leave real early in the morning."

The discussion ended when Mom's water broke. Dad and Cliff put air in a low tire and the expectant parents took off and arrived at the hospital about 11:00 p.m.

On December 3, 1946, at sunrise, their daughter was born. Dad said, "I was the happiest person in the world." They named the six-pound, fifteen-ounce wee one Valerie Faye, but the first time her daddy held her he nicknamed her Punkin, "because she looked so pudgy." It's a nickname he uses for his sister Gladys, too, and he's never called Valerie anything else. Mom wrote in an email the day Val turned sixty: "Dad and I woke up talking about you this morning, Val. The trip to the hospital in the middle of the night, our stop at May and Cliff's to stay all night, but we didn't dare. I'll never forget seeing the sun rise right after you were born and how happy we were to have our first baby with all her fingers and toes. You are still as precious to us today as you were that bright morning."

The new father had to tear himself away and get back to the ranch the next morning, because his folks had gone to Oregon for the winter to visit Bonnie and Russ, leaving him in charge. Five days later he drove back to Rapid City to collect his wife and daughter.

Mom carried their first-born into a freezing house, since no one had been at home to keep the fires burning. Dad built a fire in the coal stove, and soon, his family was cozy. The next morning he filled the boiler on the stove with water so the new mother would have hot water to wash diapers. Then he saddled a horse and went out to check on the cattle.

***

That spring after Dode and Clara returned from Oregon, Mom and five-month-old Valerie went over to the ranch house on a cold and windy day to help Grandma. She had phlebitis (inflammation of a vein) in one leg and needed help with housework.

Dode had ridden out to herd cattle in a field nearby. My dad was planting a field of flax on leased farm land about four miles away, when he noticed a cloud of dust and a pickup approaching fast. It sped up to him and stopped. A neighbor named Clara John jumped out and said, "I see smoke at your place, Orman. Doesn't look good." He looked toward the house and saw the smoke. He jumped off the tractor, ran to his pickup, and with Clara following, raced home.

When he got there he found both the ranch house and the little trailer house burned to the ground. All that remained of the trailer were blackened and distorted metal ribs and the tires. My mother and Dode stood in the yard. Clara sat in the front seat of the car, chin on her chest. Baby Punkin lay sound asleep in the back seat. Both women were weeping.

Dad moved to his wife's side and put an arm around her. "Thank God you're all OK." He murmured, "What in the hell...?"

Dode spoke first. "I saw smoke and rode home as fast as I could. All I could save was this." He held up a rifle. "I reached inside the front door and grabbed it."

Dad walked over to the car and stood by his mother, who said, "Em and I were a little chilly, so I banged on the chimney with a stove iron to loosen soot. Must've let loose a live ember to the roof. I'm so sorry..."

Mom found her voice. "We were sitting in the living room, and we heard a scratching noise. We wondered what it was. Soot and other stuff flew past the window and we realized it was fire. We grabbed Valerie and ran. Grandma asked me to try to get that." She pointed to a chest of drawers that sat upright in the dirt, a wooden box of silverware and a picture frame still standing neatly on top. She looked down at her scraped arms and wondered how she had carried the whole thing out. Her arms fell limp to her sides. "I tried to go back in, but it was too late." Swiping new tears aside, she made sooty streaks across her cheeks. "I tried pouring buckets of water on flames reaching across the grass for our house, but it was too late."

Dad took her into his arms and said again. "Oh, Honey. Thank God you're all OK."

All the two families had left of personal belongings were the contents of the chest of drawers, the clothes on their backs, and the clothes that Mom had hung on the clothesline that morning. She wrote later in her life story *Prairie Rattlers, Long Johns, and Chokecherry Wine* (PublishAmerica, 2003): "People came from miles around, bringing clothing, bedding and food to tide us over until we could get established again. The next morning, seven neighbors drove their tractors to the field and finished seeding the flax. Later, women held showers for me and Grandma to replace household things and things for the baby." Andy Thybo, the ranch owner, moved in a one-bedroom house for Dode and Clara, and a neighbor towed a sheep wagon into the yard for Mom, Dad, and Valerie. Though this doesn't sound like upscale living, sheep wagons could be seen as the forerunners of camping trailers of today with well-designed sleeping and cooking spaces. Grateful to have it, my parents soon discovered it leaked though and they had to be careful where they set the baby basket.

As if the fire hadn't been discouraging enough, that summer my dad began to have problems with allergies. Every night he came in from the fields with swollen and watery eyes. One night his eyes had swollen nearly shut, and he had trouble breathing. He sat down at the supper table and said, "I'm not sure I can keep on with this ranching and farming."

9

Flyboy

1950: The average annual salary in the U.S. is
$3,815 per year
1952: Dwight D. Eisenhower becomes president
1953: A Ford sedan can be purchased for
$1,900, a loaf of bread for 17 cents, a
dozen eggs for 58 cents
1954: On the Waterfront *with Marlon Brando*
wins Best Picture at the Academy Awards and
Kitty Kallen has a hit song with "Little
Things Mean a Lot"

With some regret, but looking forward to life without
hay fever, my dad once again said goodbye to ranch life.
He left his cattle in Dode's care and moved back to Rapid
City which still bustled with post-war growth and job
opportunities. Old friends Ray and Esther Shepherd from
Fort Peck days offered lodging for Dad, Mom and baby,
until he and Mom could find their own place. The two
families lived together for about two weeks, until my

parents moved to the Bradsky house on Highway 79. After that they rented an older two-bedroom house on the edge of Caputa, a little town twelve miles east of Rapid City. Dad found a job delivering fuel for Puritan Oil. He said, "There was no shortage of jobs if you weren't too picky."

When asked about his memories of Valerie's toddlerhood, Dad told about the time she once ran to him screaming. Neither he nor Mom could find any wounds, scrapes or bruises anywhere. Later, Dad found a scorched bobby pin sticking out of an electric wall outlet and realized what had happened.

Em, Orm and Valerie

When Valerie was nine months old, Mom found she was pregnant again, and she and Dad happily went about readying their house and lives for two babies. One day Mom went into the kitchen to start supper and set Valerie on the floor to play. While she peeled potatoes at the sink, she felt something sliding around her ankle. She looked down. A blue racer snake about three feet long and an inch and a half thick had wrapped itself around her ankle. She screamed, kicked it off, and reached for her baby. Not being a believer in old wives' tales, one popped into her mind anyway: a pregnant woman's baby would be born with a mole in the shape of something that frightened her.

When Dad got home, he got an earful of snake news. He had to admit he'd seen one or two in the basement. But he hadn't said anything and had gotten rid of them, hoping that would be the end of it. He conducted a thorough search for holes where snakes might enter the house, plugged them, and told Mom he considered the problem solved.

In the summer of 1948, on June 16 just after midnight, Mom gave birth to me, Alyce Marlene, with not a snake-shaped mole anywhere. Dad told me, "You were so little, you just looked like a little stinker." He calls me Stinker to this day, the only person in the world who will ever get away with it. I spent a few years wishing he wouldn't, but am now thankful he's still here to say, "Hey Stinker," when he answers the phone and hears my voice. When I asked him how he felt when he found he had a second daughter, he said, "I was so proud to have another little baby in the crib upstairs."

Valerie, a proud daddy, Marlene

Unfortunately, the snakes kept slithering through the Caputa house, and Mom could never let her babies play on the floor. One morning a noise outside the bedroom window woke her. She sat up and saw her husband hurrying away from the house with yet another dead snake dangling from his hand.

They found a remodeled garage with one bedroom to move into until they could find something bigger. Not long after that they found a two-bedroom remodeled garage and then a house on Adams Street that they had to vacate temporarily to fumigate for bedbugs. Eventually, from there they moved to Maple Street.

By then my dad had become the manager of a service station, a job he held for several years. In 1950, he got a job at the Milwaukee Railroad, where he took tickets, managed schedules, and "whatever they needed doing." He like the work, but when the company wanted him to transfer to Pierre, he quit and, while waiting for something better, got a job taking census in Pennington County. Another time he went into business with a man and bought land and leased the oil and mineral rights to it.

He always took time off from work to go hunting in the fall. My mother went hunting with him in later years, but earlier in the marriage, it was something Dad did with his brothers and friends. They spent days planning their outing and getting their rifles cleaned and then happily loaded their pickups to head for deer camp.

Along about February of 1950, Mom became pregnant again. By that fall during deer hunting season, she had grown huge and found it hard to keep up with two little girls—I was about eighteen months old and my sister about three years old. But Mom could not convince her husband to stay home from his hunting trip. After all, he had already promised his buddies and made plans and said, "Don't worry. I'll call from deer camp in a day or two. Won't take me long to get home if you need me." And off he went.

When he called later, his wife told him her hip kept going out on her. He hurried home and when he got there called the doctor, who told them to get to the hospital for induced labor. But the birth progressed on its own, and on November 18, 1950, my parents welcomed a third healthy baby, making it a family of five.

"We were so surprised it was a boy," said my dad. "We hadn't even picked out a boy's name." They talked it over and soon settled on Orman Ray. Dad could hardly wait to call his parents, who were again in Oregon that winter. For fun, the pregnancy had somehow been kept secret from them, so when Clara heard she had a new grandson, Dad got a kick out of her saying, "Oh, my Lord!"

Mom said my dad went around passing out cigars and smugly telling everyone, "Anybody can make a girl because you have the pattern in front of you, but not everybody can make a boy." He nicknamed his son Butch, a name he liked the sound of and that his cousin Howard used for his son. Dad took his two daughters "out north" (the homestead country in Perkins County where he and Mom grew up) to stay with their Aunt May and Uncle Cliff until Mom and son got out of the hospital.

I believe this is my earliest memory: mom walks into a dim room holding a bundle to her chest. She lays it on a bed, opens a pale blue blanket, and smiles at Val and me. "Here is your new little brother." Later, probably a few days (this I don't remember), we both got peed on while watching him have a bath. Mom says we never wanted to help much after that.

When Butch, or Ormie Ray as others in the family called him, grew old enough, his daddy liked to take him along on errands. Butch was a shy little boy. Dad said, "I took him everywhere with me, and I can still feel him clinging to my pant leg when I talked to someone he didn't know." Dad once saw a John Deere pedal toy tractor in a store window and talked the owner out of it for a twenty-dollar bill. "Butch took right off on it," Dad said, "and rode it for miles around the yard."

Punkin, Butch, and Stinker

Even now my dad's eyes light up if a toddler runs by in a restaurant or on the street and especially when his great grandchildren visit. He connects easily with little people, often quipping things like "Where'd you get that hat," or tickling a tummy to make them laugh. At the age of seventy Dad said that if he had it to do over, he would have had more children, because he enjoyed them so much.

But in the 1950s, after having three children in four years, my parents talked it over and decided three was enough. My dad must have known a guy who knew a guy, because he arranged to have an illegal vasectomy.

A family of five needed more room, so my parents moved again, this time buying a bigger house on Elmhurst Drive. They remodeled the upstairs for kids' bedrooms and talked about eventually building a new house on the empty lot next door. While living in that house, I stuck my hand into a push mower and had to get stitches in one finger. That bad memory is balanced by the one of Dad making pancakes for me and my brother and sister on a Saturday morning so Mom could sleep in. We sat barefooted in our pajamas around a Formica-topped chrome-legged table, while Dad, dishtowel tucked into his belt for an apron, turned flapjacks with a deft jerk of the skillet and no pancake turner. He said, "Are you ready for a pannygoogle?" just to hear us giggle. Later when he had grandchildren, Dad often had at least one standing on a stool to help stir the pannygoogle batter.

My mother loved that house and neighborhood, and expected to raise her family there. However, one day the phone rang. When she answered, she found herself talking to a realtor, who wanted to bring people to look at the house. Her husband had listed it without telling her, and on top of that, he had listed it including all of her furniture. They ended up selling the house "lock, stock and barrel," as she called it, but when it came time to meet with the realtor to finalize the deal, she waited an extra beat to sign, thinking that would let everyone know that she had not been consulted. Whether or not anyone else in the room got it, Dad did. From then on, he became more careful about talking to her before making decisions of that scale.

I asked him to tell me his version of that story: "That realtor moved so fast I didn't have a chance to tell your mother about my plans. I wanted to surprise her with a brand new house and all new furniture." He had already bought a two-bedroom brick house being built in a new development on 44th Street in the South Canyon area of Rapid City. However, he had to move his family into a basement apartment while waiting for the home to be finished.

***

In the fall of 1954 when hunting season rolled around again, my dad took time off to go grouse hunting with friends. They drove north to Mud Butte and then east about five miles. Leaving vehicles parked, they walked up a draw and came to a fence they had to crawl through. As my dad bent over to take his turn, he heard a gunshot. Pain seared into his left arm. He fell to the ground.

A hunter walking behind him had stumbled and accidentally fired his shotgun.

Someone in the hunting party sped my dad to Faith, the nearest town with a doctor. But when surgery seemed likely, someone else with an airplane flew him to Rapid City. When Mom received a phone call that he would be arriving at the Rapid City airport, she called her brother-in-law Aldy, who drove her to the airport. They got there in time to see the little plane land, helped my dad into the back seat of the car, and sped to the hospital "laying on the horn" all the way. Mom said she knew Dad's injuries must be serious because he looked so white. In surgery, doctors saved his left arm where most of the pellets had lodged, and removed nineteen from his back. He spent about a week in the hospital, and even now, over fifty years later, an x-ray reveals pellets in Dad's back. He still has a few in his arm and is happy to show you how they roll around under his skin. The man who shot him helped pay the bill and remained a close friend and poker buddy for many years.

***

For his work in the oil business, Dad often traveled to Wyoming, so when he found he could trade his cattle for a used 1948 Aeronca Champ airplane complete with flying lessons, he went for it. Not only was the plane handy for business, he used it to travel "out north" to help his parents set up a retirement house in Prairie City. (In 1955, most of the old town of Strool was renamed Prairie City and picked up and moved two miles north so it would be on paved Highway 8.)

My dad also had a lot of fun with his airplane. My mother says that's when her hair started going gray. Dad took all of us for rides, but not together, for the plane was too small. On the day it was my turn, Dad strapped Val and me side by side into the back seat and off we went. I strained against the seat belt to raise myself high enough to see out the window, where I saw green grass, trees and hills that looked so pretty from way up high. Another time Dad took Mom, with Butch sitting between her legs, to Edgemont, about sixty miles south of Rapid, to visit her brother Bill and his wife.

One day he flew my cousin Carol's husband Chuck Breidenbach over to the Badlands east of Rapid to hunt coyotes. But circling the plane to get closer and closer to the prey made Chuck sick. Finally Chuck said, "You'd better set this thing down, Ormie, or I'll mess it up good." In his haste to land, Dad touched one wing to the ground. Luckily damage was light enough that they were able to take off. They made it home—without any coyotes.

On trips out north Dad often flew over his brother-in-law Carl Ruby's ranch, dipping his wings in greeting. Carl always waved back. One day Carl and his wife Ruth stopped at our house and got out of the car asking, "Is Ormie OK?"

"He's fine," said Mom. "Why?"

Carl explained that the day before he had seen Dad's plane hit a high wire near his ranch. Funny, Dad had never mentioned that.

I asked Dad if Dakota winds or storms ever added interest to flying a small plane. He said, "A couple of times I couldn't tell if I was upside down or right side up if I flew into big clouds. I was supposed to stay under them. And I ran out of daylight a time or two." His plane was not equipped with lights. He eventually realized the plane was too expensive and said, "I traded it straight across for a dump truck, something I could make money with."

***

In the South Canyon neighborhood of Rapid City, all of the brick houses with white trim looked alike. Dads went to work, moms drank coffee and chatted across back fences, and kids walked to school. After school and on weekends my siblings and I and the neighborhood kids raced trikes and bikes and roller skates up and down the sidewalks. Dad put up a swing set in our back yard, but perhaps it attracted too many kids.

Mom often found herself in charge of other little boys in the neighborhood. "What a production," she said, "when they all came in the house for a drink of water." She was not pleased the day one little boy came over and announced that he had been told to come to our house while his mother went to work.

Another day after my sister and I had left for school and Butch had gone outside to play, Mom looked out her kitchen window while doing the breakfast dishes. She counted nineteen little boys in her yard.

That night when Dad got home, she said, "You know, Honey, maybe it's time we start looking for a place in the country to raise our kids."

Butch, Marlene, and Valerie in 1953

Family of five, 1954

10

Country Dad

1957: April Love *by Pat Boone shares top song list*
with All Shook Up *by Elvis Presley*
Gas is 31 cents a gallon and the average annual
income is $5,443
1960: Gunsmoke *and* The Ed Sullivan Show *are*
popular TV shows
Gas is 31 cents a gallon and the average annual
income is $6,227
1963: President John F. Kennedy is assassinated
1965: The Beatles dominate the song charts, gas is
31 cents a gallon and average annual income
is $7,704

My dad liked the idea of moving his family to the
country, and had even heard of a place he wanted to check
out. He stopped to see it one day while out on business and
liked it so much he wanted to show it to Mom.

Driving Mom's 1954 blue and white Chevy sedan, they
headed west from Sturgis to Deadwood on Highway 14A,

winding through Boulder Canyon in the Black Hills National Forest. Alongside the highway, Bear Butte Creek splashed over and around boulders, and in a few places the highway curved into deep shade under sheer rock walls. About six miles from Sturgis, the canyon opened and became a valley. On the right side of the highway a golf course spread toward rolling hills beyond, and on the left, a few homes on one- and two-acre lots scattered across a wide clearing bordered by a forest of pines.

After passing a white schoolhouse, Dad turned left and followed a two-track lane that curved through Ponderosa, jack and lodgepole pine trees, some a hundred and fifty feet tall. He parked in the graveled clearing in front of the house and got out. More trees stood about the house and on nearby grassy knolls.

"See those trailers?" he said. Downhill from the house sat two. "There are five more trailer spaces, and if we get them filled, the rent income would help us make payments on the place." Slowly turning to the right in a circle, he pointed out a barn with fenced corral and loading chute, a fenced pasture bordered by a canyon that dropped off about a hundred yards from the house, and nearer the house a single-car garage and shop. Looking west uphill from the house, he said, "There's a pump house and well up there, and just beyond is a rock quarry. A hundred and forty acres all together."

Mom scrolled a look around. "This is like a park. The kids would love it here."

"Honey, I think we'd all love it here." Dad smiled.

Mom faced the house and frowned. "Well, let's take a look at that old house." It had the look of a log cabin with vertical barked siding made of curved-on-one-side slices of tree trunks. They walked up to the door, climbed two steps made from rock slabs, and opened the screen door. This later addition to the east side of the house had wall-to-wall casement windows and two rooms—the sunroom-like entry and a small bedroom on the north end. Another step up took them into the central part of the house that had begun life as a schoolhouse. Now it was two rooms—a kitchen with a combination wood and electric stove and low sink in one dark corner—and a living room with a wood stove that seemed to take up half of the room. Two bedrooms with a walk-through bathroom between (shower only, no tub) had been added to the west side of the house.

On the drive back to Rapid City, Dad noticed Mom wasn't saying much. Finally he said, "What do you think?"

"The house is old, but it's big enough," she said. "We could have cows and chickens, even a garden. I could grow vegetables and can them just like my mother did."

"There's even a cellar to store them in. You could churn butter if you want to."

"The kids could help. They should have chores like we did when we were kids."

Dad smiled and said, "I like the country school, and the kids could walk to it."

So, in 1956 when I was eight years old, they made the deal and moved once again. Mom designed and hand painted a sign to advertise Boulder Canyon Trailer Park, and Dad installed it at the end of our lane next to the highway. Before long, all seven trailer spaces were rented. A little later, Dad and a neighbor remodeled the kitchen by adding more cupboards, moving the sink under a window, and moving a doorway, which made room for a dining nook.

Tourism had already become a big part of the economy in the Black Hills. During the summer, people driving by on their way to Deadwood, Mount Rushmore, or Spearfish Canyon often stopped by our place to ask if they could pitch tents in the shady park-like area between the house and the highway. Mom and Dad said sure and didn't charge anything, but later, when campers began leaving too much trash behind, they started charging a dollar a night.

Dad continued to work in the oil business, but worked hard at home, too. Soon, he and Mom got the idea to develop the campground business even more, hoping to build the business enough so that Dad could stay home and work full time. If they provided restrooms and showers, they could charge more, so Dad built another building, adding laundry facilities for the renters and the campers. Mom painted a new sign for the highway: Boulder Park Trailer Court & Campground.

I didn't know it then, but ours was the traditional gender-biased household of the fifties. Mom and Dad expected my sister and me to help clean house, do laundry and wash dishes, while our brother worked outdoors with Dad. When he was older, Butch mowed all of the lawns around the house and campground, and I did that a few times, too. I learned to drive the summer that Dad let Butch and me use an old red and white pickup truck with automatic transmission to haul piles of pine needles a quarter mile to the rock quarry. We couldn't wait to get another pile of needles raked and loaded, so we could take turns driving. It is only now that I suspect Dad had it figured that way.

That house in the country holds lots of memories that remind me of the kind of dad I was blessed with as a kid. When I wondered what to be when I grew up, I talked it over with Dad one day. He said, "You can be anything you want." The confidence in his voice made me believe I could and that he thought I was smart and capable of doing it, whatever I decided. When I was about ten, I asked him one afternoon, "Am I pretty?" He enclosed me in his arms and said, "Stinker, you're the prettiest girl in the world." I knew he could be just a little biased and would tell my sister the same, but I liked hearing it anyway. The hug felt great, too.

Living in the country, my siblings and I had the freedom to roam in safety. Because we watched Hopalong Cassidy, Roy Rogers, Gene Autry and The Lone Ranger on TV, we liked to play Cowboys and Indians, and our playground looked a lot like the landscapes we saw on TV. Out by the garage there was a pile of lath for fencing, where we could grab a new "horse" whenever we needed one. We "rode" to the canyon and climbed down big rock steps to the bottom looking for bandits or their hideouts. I wonder now if Dad ever headed for that pile of lath intending to use it and puzzled about whatever happened to it.

One day Dad brought home a real horse, a white one named Princess. He said, "You can ride her any time you want," and showed us how to boost each other onto her bare back. She was so gentle she would let us crawl under her belly.

Often, our country dogs got run over on the highway, and we moped for days. Finally, Mom declared, "No more dogs." However, that Christmas, our cousin Carol and her husband Chuck Breidenbach dropped by with a small ball of gray and black fur with a red bow around his neck. Three kids fell instantly in love with a Norwegian elkhound puppy, so we got to keep him. His official name was Hindsdale Tiny Tim, because he was the runt of the litter, but we always called him Timmy. Dad would step out of the house, find Timmy sunning himself on the step, and bend down to scratch his ears and rub his back crooning, "Hey there, Fat Boy," teasing Timmy about his life of leisure. Dad built Timmy a doghouse using a sheet of metal from an old clothes dryer for the roof. But after lightning struck it once while Timmy was inside, he never went into it again. Timmy was smart enough to stay off the highway and lived long after all of us kids left home.

We had lots of company in Boulder Canyon, especially on summer weekends, when relatives and friends stopped by. Dad and Mom usually invited people to stay for supper. After all the serving bowls were on the table, and people had found a chair and scooted in, Dad would say, "Grab a root and growl."

Later, as people climbed into their cars for departure, windows would be rolled down for one last remark, and Dad would tell the driver, "Don't take any wooden nickels," or "Watch out for the guy behind the guy in front of you."

Summers also meant playing hide-and-go-seek until after dark and running barefoot through mud puddles and little piles of hailstones after a thunderstorm. In spring, we first found crocuses sprinkled in the grass (sometimes poking up through snow), and then buttercups, bluebells and shooting stars appeared among the grass and milkweed.

Living in a forest meant the possibility of forest fires. Once when Dad was gone on a job, the county sheriff knocked on the door and told us to evacuate, because a forest fire near Deadwood was headed our way. Mom told us to each pack a couple of changes of clothes and a favorite toy. By the time she packed clothes, important papers, a few photos and her brand new Singer sewing machine, we kids were sitting in the car with Timmy and two cats, Spunky and Blondie. Mom jumped in and drove down to the school to pick up Miss Thomas, because she didn't have a car, but the teacher had heard on the radio that the winds had changed, so we went back home, the adventure over.

After the bustle of summer, winter became much quieter family time. We spent many nights with wind whistling around the windows playing card games (Oh Heck, Twenty-One), putting together jigsaw puzzles on a card table set up in the living room by the stove and TV, or reading newspapers or books.

One morning we awoke to find the house darker and quieter than usual. We tried to look out the windows but found the ones on the north side nearly covered with snow, and it had piled three-quarters of the way up the front door. Dad had to shovel his way to the garage and barn and says, "That was the time I had to do chores in my hip boots." We kids bundled up and hurried outside, following the tunnels Dad had dug, and found snowdrifts curled as high as the eaves on the west side of the house.

Another winter after about two feet of fresh snow had fallen overnight, Mom got up to make breakfast. We kids were still in bed, and Dad had already gone out. Each morning he walked up to the pump house to turn on the pump and then went down to the barn to milk the cow. As Mom dropped slices of bacon into a frying pan, she glanced out the kitchen window and saw Dad speed by on our sled. One of us kids walked into the kitchen and said, "Was that Dad?"

When Dad came into the house later with a pail full of warm milk, Mom said, "Who did we buy that sled for, Honey?"

Dad smiled and said, "Best way I know of to get from the pump house to the barn in snow like this." We could grab the rope of our sled and drag it up the hill to the pump house, jump on, and slide past the house, past the trailers, and almost to the school.

Making snow angels was my favorite thing to do after a fresh snowfall. We'd race into our coats, scarves, mittens and overshoes, trying to be the first one out. I can still feel the cold creeping into my back as I lay in soft fluffy snow, sliding my legs from side to side and my arms up and down. After one last look at the dark silhouettes of snowflakes falling toward my face, I sat up—gently, without making a sitzmark—reached one foot as far away as possible, and hopped away, so that it looked like the snow angel had magically appeared.

However, snow measured in feet was unusual, and we could usually get to town all winter. We spent one winter going bowling in Sturgis once a week. After Dad had taken it up and joined a league, he thought bowling would be fun for all of us. He patiently taught each of us how to step forward to deliver the ball and line it up with marks on the wood lane. And he and Mom cheered whenever we knocked down a few pins or got a spare or strike.

Our family took many two-hour car trips out north to visit Grandpa and Grandma Willey in Prairie City, May and Cliff and cousins Bonnie and Dennis in Buffalo, and relatives and friends in Rapid. We often sang songs along the way. Mom and Dad would sing "Sentimental Journey," and "Take Me Back to the Black Hills," with harmony, and they taught us many other songs, especially Christmas carols. We usually spent Christmas Day with my uncle Aldy and his family either in Rapid or at our house.

We tried to keep Christmas Eve to ourselves. After supper, usually oyster stew, Val and I had to wash the dishes, and then we got to open our presents. The next morning we would find something amazing under the Christmas tree, like a doll we had seen in the "Wish Book" (Sears catalog), somehow delivered by "Santa" though we had no fireplace.

In 1959, at the age of 84, my grandpa Dode Willey died, so we had to take a sad car trip to Prairie City for his funeral. In church that day, I saw something I had never seen before that shocked and worried me—tears running down my dad's face and him swiping at them with a white handkerchief. Not long after, Grandma Clara moved to Hillsboro, Oregon, where she lived with her daughter Bonnie until the age of 93 in 1985.

The campground and trailer park business didn't bring in enough money, and Dad took to calling it the Poorfarm. He often found other jobs that fit his schedule. One involved grading minutemen missile sites east of Sturgis. After the nuclear missiles had been installed in underground silos, Dad took his equipment to each one and graded the earth around it. Also during those years, he sold mutual funds and was so successful that he won two trips to conventions in Las Vegas for him and Mom.

In the spring of 1965, Dad built a large room and covered porch onto the north side of the house, so Mom could open a small grocery store. It was a good opportunity to add a second bathroom, and my sister Val and I, teenagers by then, were excited to find out we would soon have a bathtub. Also during the remodel, Dad removed the old log siding from the house and garage and replaced it with horizontal board siding. Val and I spent that summer brushing barn-red paint onto rough boards and later trying to get it off ourselves with turpentine.

Dad quit smoking in about 1964. He went cold turkey after nearly wrecking the car once when live embers landed between his legs. He was trying to brush them away when he looked up and saw that he was headed straight for the concrete abutment of a bridge. He took the cigarettes out of his shirt pocket, tossed them, and never smoked again.

At some point Dad traded part of the Boulder Park acreage for the surveying of forty acres deeper in the forest. Then he used a road grader and built roads to the new area so he could sell lots. Over the next few years, people bought lots and built homes there, and the last time I drove through, I found that Willey Lane is still there.

Because Dad traveled a lot, discipline fell to Mom most. She said, "When your dad came home from business trips, he was so tickled to see you kids he spent a lot of time playing with you." He sometimes let us do things Mom had already said no about, so they soon had to have a talk about that. But Dad rarely punished us physically. Val wrote in a family memory book in 1988: "I remember how loving and caring Dad was, always supportive and there for me. He wasn't real strict, but had a special way of letting me know when things weren't right."

Butch wrote: "I was about 8 or 9 years old and we lived

in Boulder Canyon. I was pouring gas on the garage floor and lighting it. Bad, bad thing to be doing. He took me in the house, sat me down with the leather strap in hand. He asked me if I thought I deserved the strap. Boy, did I say the right thing. 'Yes, I deserve it.' Then he said, 'If you realize the seriousness of what you did, I won't use this strap.'"

He did use the strap on me, and my story has to do with fire too. I had sneaked a strictly forbidden book of matches and was playing Going Camping with the neighbor kids, when we accidentally let our campfire in the pasture spread to a large pile of brush. One of the kids ran home and told his mom, who must have called the fire department. A big red truck arrived and put the fire out. I was lucky that no one was hurt and that the brush pile was some distance from buildings or big trees. That night Dad spanked me with the strap and sent me to my room with no supper. I don't remember going without food, but I do remember the strap, the only spanking I remember getting from Dad.

Fast forward to my teen years: One night after getting all gussied up, I was hanging out in the living room keeping an eye out the window for my date's car, when Dad suddenly stood up, reached into his pocket and pulled out a handful of change. Smooshing the coins around in his hand, he fished out a dime and handed it to me. "Keep this in your purse," he said. "If you ever end up some place you don't want to be and need a ride, call me. Any place, any time, just call me. OK? Promise me."

I said, "Thanks, Dad," and dropped the dime into my purse, doubting I'd ever need it. I never did, but knowing Dad would jump out of bed in the middle of the night to rescue me made that emergency dime feel like gold. And it made me love my dad to pieces.

When she was a junior in high school, Val started going

out with an airman from Ellsworth Air Force Base. He soon brought a friend so we could double date a few times. Dad seemed a little nervous about our "flyboys," and continued to make sure we had our dimes when we left on dates. He insisted we be home by midnight.

One night we spotted our dates' car turning off the highway and scurried about for our purses and coats. Before we could go out the door, Dad blurted, "Keep your knees together and you'll stay out of trouble." It embarrassed me, but I knew it was hard for him to say and he said it anyway because we were important to him. It was a great gift for a parent to give a child, a father to give a daughter.

After graduating from high school in 1965, Val opted for business college in Rapid City, and a year later I graduated and enrolled at the South Dakota School of Mines in Rapid. We rented an apartment in the basement of a house near campus and became so busy going to school, working and dating that we rarely made it home, even on weekends.

By 1966, Butch was a sophomore in high school. He still helped Mom run the campground and store, but she knew he wouldn't be there for long. Dad traveled more and more with sales work. They talked it over and decided to sell the Poorfarm and move back to Rapid City. My parents moved a lot, but Boulder Park is one place they stayed for a decade, and I consider myself lucky to have grown up there.

Within two years of selling the campground, Mom and Dad's son would graduate from high school, both daughters would marry, and they would become grandparents.

11

Granddad and Great

In 1966, Orm and Em bought a three-bedroom split-level house in the South Canyon area of Rapid City, only a few streets away from the new brick home they had left to raise their kids in the country. Butch enrolled as a junior at Rapid City High School.

One day my big sister came home and surprised us all by saying, "I'm getting married."

"What?" Dad said. "You're way too young, Punks." Val was 19, but she and her boyfriend Marlyn Stubbe, a student at the South Dakota School of Mines in Rapid City, were expecting a baby. So, in October of 1966, Dad walked Val down the aisle. I was her Maid of Honor.

Several months later, Dad rushed to the hospital one evening to wait with Mom and his son-in-law for news about the birth of their first grandchild. Soon, my parents welcomed another baby girl into their lives—Jennie Lynn. Mom later wrote, "She looked so much like Valerie right after her birth, it seemed like the same thing happening as nineteen years before, except roles had been switched."

I was a freshman at the School of Mines in Rapid, and

because Mom and Dad had moved to town, I moved home to save money. The summer before in the college library where I worked part-time, I had met a tall skinny graduate student named Norm Johnson. One day, as I checked out books for him at the circulation desk, he asked me to a movie. We began dating steadily, got engaged, and Norm had an old-fashioned talk with Dad to "ask for my hand." At our wedding in June of 1967, less than a year after walking his elder daughter down the aisle, Dad offered his elbow to me. My new husband accepted a job in Richland, Washington, that became our destination on a road-trip honeymoon.

Meanwhile, my dad continued to do well selling mutual funds and insurance. Mom, having nearly raised her family, decided to look for work, too, and found a job doing machine embroidery that she enjoyed.

Just before Christmas that year, Dad got a call from his boss, who, after offering him a job as division manager in Colorado, asked, "Can you be in Grand Junction by January first?" Mom and Dad had been in their house only a year, and Mom hated to move away from her grandchild or give up her job, but they couldn't pass up a good promotion. So, they sold the house, and after the traditional Christmas dinner at Uncle Aldy's, struck out for Colorado; Dad and Mom in the car, and Butch, with Timmy the dog riding shotgun, in the pickup on a long, cold and snowy trip south and west.

In his new job, Dad recruited and doubled the sales force and sales of the company, and Mom arranged monthly lunches for business meetings and did the bookkeeping. In a round-robin letter to his family in those years Dad wrote:

"I am still with Waddell & Reed selling

mutual funds and insurance. Had a fairly
good year considering some of the time was
spent hiring and training men. I now have
five besides myself here on the Western
Slope. My goal for a full division is ten full
time men or women. Hope to accomplish
this by 1973."

My parents occupied four different homes in
Colorado—a large four-bedroom rental, a mobile home that
they purchased in a nice park, a small house they bought to
fix up and resell, and finally, a red ranch house with large
yards and garden space on the edge of town. During fall
seasons, Dad and Butch enjoyed many elk and deer hunting
trips, but when it came to fishing, Mom grabbed her fishing
pole, too, and they all headed for the Colorado and
Gunnison Rivers in search of catfish and trout.

Thinking that Colorado would provide a beautiful
setting in which to revive the Willey Family Reunion, in
the summer of 1968 my parents invited relatives from
South Dakota, Oregon and California to rented cabins on
Grand Mesa. Everyone parked their tents and camping
trailers in the yard and got reacquainted. Sixty-five people
showed up, including Clara, Dad's mother, by then age 78.

Mom and Dad's first granddaughter Jennie Lynn soon
had a sibling and cousins. Val's second child, Todd
Marlyn, was born in March of 1970. In September of the
same year, I gave birth to my first child, Eric Norman. By
the age of 53 my dad was the grandfather of three. He
wrote in another Willey robin letter:

"First off want to tell of our wonderful
wonderful Xmas. Of course the highlights
were those little grandchildren one of which

we met for the first time (Eric). He is such a cute little guy as are the others also. We didn't spoil them either, (much). How can you keep from it? We can't. They all left for home on the 30th and were all safely home by the 31st."

Back in the olden days before computers and email, Mom always sent birthday cards to everyone in the family. Sometimes she asked Dad to help out, and in 1994 he wrote in my card, (his emphasis) "Dear Marlene, what a perfect time to tell you how wonderful it is to have a daughter like you. You have made me <u>so</u> proud <u>so</u> many times it is no wonder why every time I see you the hugs and squeezes are just automatic."

***

In 1973, my parents had a rough year, losing Dad's younger brother Aldy, age 52, to cancer, Mom's brother-in-law Cliff (best man at their wedding) to a house fire, and Mom's brother Richard to heart disease.

Dad and Mom, at ages 56 and 53, began to wonder if they should wait until any "official" retirement age to quit working. By 1976 when Butch had graduated from high school, enrolled in college, and moved to his own apartment, my parents decided they were ready. So, they quit their jobs, sold their house, bought a 24-foot Terry travel trailer, loaded it with groceries and fishing gear, and hit the road. They planned to see all fifty states. If necessary, they would stop along the way and get jobs to make travel money to keep savings intact.

Mom called this their "first retirement" and described their adventures in *Beyond the Silent Prairie*. As they saw the sights and fished the lakes and rivers, they covered over 28,000 miles.

They visited my family in San Jose, California, which by then included Norm's and my second son, Ryan Scott. They stopped in Denver to see Val and family, and timed it so they would be in Rock Springs, Wyoming, in June of 1977 for Butch's wedding to Katie Viens—again; Dad gave away the bride, because Katie's parents could not attend.

In 1978 Butch and Katie had a son named Jesse Ray and in 1980 a daughter Kristamae, making six grandchildren for Mom and Dad.

At about the age of sixty, Dad began to have intermittent trouble with equilibrium and dizzy spells. So, while traveling through Oregon in the late 1970s, he stopped at the veteran's hospital in Portland for a thorough checkup. Doctors didn't identify specific reasons for the symptoms, and though relieved, Dad decided to get off the road, at least for a while. He and Mom have lived in Oregon ever since. My cousin Boyd Ruby offered them a caretaker's job and apartment at an RV rental and storage facility he owned in North Plains, and they moved in. After that place sold, they both worked for my cousin Carol and her husband Chuck in their sign company in Wilsonville, until they decided to start their own sign company in Eugene with my brother and his wife.

Until recent years, my parents always kept a camping trailer or motor home parked in the driveway for getting to those hunting and fishing spots on weekends. Also, during several winters they did the snowbird thing with Dad wrangling their RV to California, Texas and the Southwest.

Dad often said he "couldn't get the hang of retirement." When he got bored or wanted extra money, he went out to find a job. He worked as a greeter at K-Mart, a security guard at a sugar plant in Texas, and a maintenance man and gardener at an apartment complex, to name a few. After a move to Roseburg to be near its veteran's medical center, he began volunteering at the golf shack on the VA hospital grounds, which had the fringe benefit of free use of the golf course. Golf became the cowboy's new sport of choice, and about three times a week he met his buddies to "chase those little white balls." One day Dad came home from golfing, and when Mom asked how the game went, he said, "None of us could hit a bull in the ass with a scoop."

My mother had a heart attack in 1981 but recovered well and in her 70s struck up a new career designing and selling doily and craft patterns in national magazines. From there she moved to writing and published many articles and two books. Eventually, macular degeneration took away her central vision, so crocheting and writing became more difficult, but she continued to write stories and poetry. Special programs on her computer allow her to use gigantic fonts so she can still read send e-mails every day. In recent years she has had intermittent problems with atrial fibrillation and congestive heart condition which sometimes lands her in the hospital.

Dad has spent many hours at her bedside, always on hand just to talk or get things she needs. Once, I arrived in time to take Mom home from the hospital. After we got her settled into her chair, Dad said, "Things just don't work right when she's not here."

In the spring of 2008 he probably saved her life.

After getting the flu and bronchitis, my mother became dehydrated and could not keep anything down, including antibiotics. She wanted to stay in bed, but Dad insisted she get up and keep her muscles working. He fed her soup whether she wanted it or not until she got her strength back.

Dad told me once that the first thing he does every morning before getting out of bed is glance over at Mom's bed. He said, "You like to see those covers movin' up and down." Mom told me the first thing she does every morning upon awakening is to listen for sounds from Dad's bed. She, who has been married to the man for over sixty-five years, wrote: "He's the cowboy I sang about on the prairie, my scalawag, rapscallion and rascal. He's my sweetheart, husband and father to my children, and most of all my friend."

Dad's problem with equilibrium worsened gradually over the years, until in 2006, after agonizing about it, he finally gave up chasing the little white balls on the golf course. The last straw came the day he fell while playing and cut his hand so deeply that it needed stitches. He reluctantly sold his golf cart and clubs and now goes nowhere without his trusty walker. The use of a cane first and then a walker did not come easily for this man who spent a lifetime with the strength and grace of a natural athlete. Those traits prevented him from getting hurt during several tumbles he has taken. He rolls with them, and except for once last winter when weakened by the flu, he always picks himself up, dusts himself off, and keeps moving. A fallen cowboy always gets back on his horse. Last summer he even had fun with the walker, letting his great granddaughter Emma sit on the seat while he wheeled her to the dining room.

The arrival of great-grandchildren brought a whole new batch of joys to a man who loves children. Val has two grands; Emma Corinne (age 10) and Olivia Grace (6), as well as four step-grands (Amanda, Samantha, Terry III, and Megan), who came with her new husband Terry McGee. (She divorced and remarried decades ago.) I have two grands; Elliot Eric (5) and Theresa Ruth (2). Dad and Mom have photos of all in a row across their coffee table, leaving room for the ones they hope to add someday.

***

The latest Willey reunion came together in the summer of 2008 in a campground near Grants Pass, Oregon, with Dad and his sister Gladys present as the elders and last surviving children of Dode and Clara Willey. People love to get them talking about the past and telling the old family stories. At these reunions, someone usually gets out a guitar and we all sing. During the latest songfest, I looked across the circle of lawn chairs and saw Dad holding hands with his grandnephew Rich Wood. Rich noticed I'd noticed, raised his and Dad's hands as one and said, "I love this guy."

***

Dad's sister Gladys once gave my parents a small tree to plant in the yard of a home they moved into, saying, "Maybe you'll stay somewhere for a while." But later Mom said with a smile, "I guess it didn't work. We are just gypsies at heart." She once counted how many times they moved and got 32. They have moved several times since.

At the ages of 90 and 87, Dad and Mom moved into a retirement center in Roseburg complete with housekeeping and three meals a day. My parents say they will not move again, and it may be true this time, because a caring and well-trained staff and friendly residents at Garden Valley Retirement Center guarantee that it lives up to its Eden-like name.

Dad's boots no longer gather dust in a corral, but step along a carpeted hallway to the dining room for chow or to play Pinochle or shoot pool with friends. From his recliner, with footrest raised and remote handy, he likes to watch rodeo cowboys, boxing, and golf tournaments on TV; read his newspapers (including the *Bison Courier* from South Dakota); and best of all, snooze.

***

My Dakota cowboy dad has spent nearly a century following the trails that called, pitching in and always doing his part, finding the fun in each day, and sharing every adventure with his sweetheart. He leaves his humble brand on three generations. He left a Dakota ranch a long time ago, but the ranch will never leave him.

Orman Othe Willey

Afterword

Orman Willey survived a rattlesnake bite, bucking broncos, a torpedo attack on his troop ship, friendly fire, German buzz bombs, and the blast of a hunter's shotgun. But a major stroke was too much. He died at the age of 91. A graveside service with military honors was held at the V.A. National Cemetery in Roseburg, Oregon, on May 27, 2009. The Dist. 12 V.F.W. Honor Guard presented Emma Willey with a flag, after which she saluted her fallen soldier during the playing of taps.

Cowboy boots found in Dad's closet

Acknowledgments

If not for my mother, Emma L. Willey, this book may never have been written. One day, I told her I was looking for a non-fiction project, and she surprised me by offering the one she was working on. She said, "Why don't you write about your dad? You can take everything I've done so far and do whatever you want with it. I know it will be good." So, I began. Thanks, Mom, for the jump-start and for the continued strong support throughout.

For years I have been meeting with a critique group affectionately known as the Peeps. At first we called ourselves Village People, because we gather in the dining room of an apartment complex named Good Samaritan Village. This quickly got shortened to Peeps, especially after the night Ken confessed to being a Marshmallow Peeps fan and to prove it, opened his shirt to reveal his official T-shirt.

With affection and great respect, I acknowledge my fellow Peeps for their valuable contributions:

Beverley Beckley, who had back surgery that included months of recovery and still read my chapters.

Carol Bosworth, the newest Peep, who brought fresh energy and gentle wisdom to my project.

Dean Sartain, who writes about history and showed me that others would be interested in my dad's history.

Donovan Reves, who became a husband, honeymooned, and still came back to read my chapters and put stickers on my pages.

Ernie Richter, who never stops asking for more details.

Jason Kilgore, who became a new father and commuted from out of town, but still squeaked in a few critiques of my chapters.

John Murphy, a fellow South Dakotan, who became a grandfather and still read my chapters.

Ken Fraundorf in memoriam, who died just as I began this project, but still had input, because sometimes as I worked, I pondered, "what would Ken say here," and I knew.

Liz Hilvers, while battling health problems, still read my chapters, pointed out the "Lizzes," and kept up Ken's tradition of applying the "smell-meter."

Martha Sargent, who flew the coop (moved away), but still read my chapters and sent encouraging notes.

Anne Warren Smith, Honorary Peep, who brought us together in her writing classes at Linn-Benton Community College and taught us how to be better writers and how to help each other be better writers.

Made in the USA